The Aboriginal Question:

Australian Racial Politics of Indigenous Recognition and Anglo De-recognition

Collected Essays Two

by Frank Salter

Social Technologies

P.O. Box 4

Ourimbah NSW 2248

Australia

E-mail: f.salter@socialtechnologies.com.au

Acknowledgment of Nation

I acknowledge Australia's first nation, founded by Christian explorers and pioneers and their descendants from Britain and other European lands.

I acknowledge Australia's first peoples, the Aborigines and Torres Strait Islanders.

And I acknowledge the Federal Commonwealth of Australia, created by the nation under the Crown to guard the liberty of all citizens.

Acknowledgments

Most of the chapters were originally published in *Quadrant* magazine, *Quadrant Online* and the Human Nature News page in my website www.socialtechnologies.com.au between 2013 and the end of 2015. Chapter six, "6 Referendum traps", was published in G. Johns (Ed.), *Recognise what? Arguments to acknowledge Aborigines, but not recognise Aboriginal culture or rights, in the Australian Constitution*. Ballarat: Connor Court. Some chapters have been lightly edited for this volume.

Table of Contents

1. Introduction

The debate over indigenous recognition in the Australian constitution might be seen as passé. After all, Noel Pearson and other indigenous leaders have declared they no longer want recognition, which they now consider to be window dressing. Instead, they want a referendum to change the Constitution to mandate an indigenous-elected advisory body attached to the Australian Parliament. This was the proposal of the Uluru Statement of mid 2017.

The "voice to parliament" would be funded largely by taxpayers unrepresented by it. This body would give advice on legislation affecting indigenous Australians, inevitably extending to every policy portfolio. It would be a racially exclusive forum, really an incipient parallel government. Its influence would be magnified by a new dedicated bureaucracy that shadowed existing departments. It would be supported by the left-controlled public broadcasters - the ABC, SBS and NITV networks - and numerous NGOs linked to the United Nations. Moreover, the national parliament would be required to consider advice proffered by the "voice", giving the latter the opportunity to pressure democratically-elected governments.

Treaties have also been floated and are presently being negotiated by the state Labor governments of Victoria and South Australia. But most public attention has been grabbed by the "voice". I discuss the origins of this proposal in chapters 10, 12, and 16. Chapter 19 describes the anti-Anglo bias of the referendum council responsible for this assault on democracy, and show that it replicates the bias of the original council ("Expert Panel") appointed by the Gillard Labor government.

Significantly, the two councils were appointed by governments ostensibly on opposite sides of politics. This illustrates the lack of policy alternatives offered to the Australian people on matters pertaining to national identity, immigration and social cohesion.

The recognition debate is still relevant because it raises or links to issues that continue to weigh on Australians' confidence and endangers their way of life and national identity. Until those issues are resolved our country will continue to be paralysed by a bad conscience about indigenous disability and confusion caused by false notions about identity and history. That paralysis lowers resistance to dangerous proposals such as a racially-based parallel government and emboldens the hostile elites responsible for them.

The Gillard government's inquiry into indigenous recognition made numerous errors of fact and procedure, errors never corrected by subsequent inquiries.

Those errors are documented in "The Misguided Case for Indigenous Recognition in the Constitution" (Chapters 3-5). Factual mistakes included the assumption that all human populations are equal in cultural and genetic endowment and the corresponding assumption that Aboriginal disability is due solely to unfair discrimination. It is wrongly assumed that when discrimination is eliminated inequality will disappear, and that indigenous Australians will be equally represented in all occupations and all levels of education. And it is wrongly assumed that until such equality is achieved, indigenous Australians will not have received fair treatment. These are all straightforward errors of fact, yet embedded in multicultural ideology and corrupt university culture.

The greatest procedural error, really an outrage, was the racially biased makeup of the expert panels appointed by governments on both sides of politics. None of these panels has included advocates of Anglo Australia, though all were filled with ethnic representatives of the indigenous and multicultural communities (Chapter 5).

The course of the debate over recognition also revealed the power of the multicultural lobby, a prime mover of the Recognise campaign (see chapters 5, 7 and 11). The same forces that express compassion for Aboriginal nationalism also seek permanent mass immigration and the criminalisation of resistance. The Aboriginal lobby is also formidable in its own right – lobby organizations, activists, a free-to-air television channel, and a generally supportive mainstream media – pushing an open-ended agenda for Aboriginal claims, and generally hostile or indifferent to the fate of white Australia.

The Recognise campaign was largely a top-down elite affair (Chapter 14). Conservative politicians such as Tony Abbott failed to show leadership (Chapter 13). Fiona McLeod SC, President of the Law Council of Australia, has called for the government to "keep faith with the important expression of self-determination, put forward in the Uluru Statement from the Heart".[1] The notion of self determination builds on the native title movement, which now covers 30 percent of the mainland. The thrust is in the direction of a separate Aboriginal nation, which Keith Windschuttle argues is already on the agenda.[2] Proposing a separate Aboriginal nation is treason, advanced by elites who also use the multicultural ethnic hierarchy to subordinate Anglo Australians and lobby for replacement-level immigration.

The anti-Anglo bias of the Recognise campaign was also shown by its assumption that only indigenous Australians deserve recognition in the constitution. This bias is already revealed in the "acknowledgment of country" ceremonies imposed on public meetings and school assemblies. These ceremonies studiously ignore the historic Anglo nation, despite our ancestors having explored, pioneered and defended the nation for its first two centuries. If the first peoples are to be recognized, how can the first nation be ignored? (Chapters 1-3).

Readers will come across biological information at many points in the book. That is because I deploy biosocial science, social analysis that draws on behavioural biology to supplement the usual sources. Biosocial information about ethnicity and race includes well-confirmed data on group differences (metabolism, work behaviour, intelligence etc.), which helps explain inequalities in health and school performance. Biosocial knowledge also sheds light on ethnic conflict and cohesion.[3]

Biological facts have been kept away from students in the social sciences since those disciplines were captured by radicals in the 1960s. The corruption began earlier in anthropology and sociology. Ignorance is the greatest cost of political correctness. Our parliamentarians and public servants are ill informed across a range of social science subjects *because* they are university graduates, not despite it. That was the thrust of my previous book, *The War on Human Nature in Australia's Political Culture* (2017).

I still believe it appropriate to acknowledge indigenous peoples. But this should be done honestly as an act of respect, not as a craven guilt reflex, not as a pretense that recognition will much change Aborigines' material circumstances, and certainly not before constitutional recognition of Australia's historic debt to our British origins and continuing European-derived core identity.

Frank Salter, May 2018.

2. Acknowledgment of Nation[*]

We acknowledge the explorers and pioneers and their descendants who planted the British flag and Christian faith on this continent, creating the Australian nation.

We acknowledge the Aboriginal and Torres Strait Islander peoples who have lived here since the Dreamtime.

And we acknowledge the Federal Commonwealth of Australia, created by the nation under the Crown to guard the liberty of all citizens.

Performance notes: Detail should be added to fit the occasion. For example, the identity and achievements of the pioneers and indigenous peoples might be elaborated, as might the functions of the Commonwealth.

---

*   Originally published in Human Nature News, www.socialtechnologies.com.au, 23 Dec. 2014.

Explanatory notes

The "Acknowledgment of Country" (AoC) ceremony purports to recognise Australia's origins but focuses exclusively on indigenous peoples. It purports to respect the traditional owners of the land but ignores the nation's sovereignty. There is no counterbalancing statement of national origins used in school assemblies or public meetings. To correct this imbalance, an Acknowledgment of Nation is suggested that supplements recognition of original indigenous habitation with acknowledgment of the origins of the Australian nation and the Federal Commonwealth it created under the crown.

In the last several years I have observed many "Acknowledgment of Country" (AoC) ceremonies. The wording varies but typically, at the start of a meeting, the master of ceremonies declares that the meeting is being held on the traditional lands of a particular indigenous people or peoples in general, describes them as the traditional custodians or owners of the land, acknowledges their close tie with the land and pays respect to their elders. I have observed versions of this ceremony at public meetings, for example at the New South Wales Parliament, in school assemblies, and on television and radio broadcasts.

My impression is that the ceremony is performed at schools and public meetings throughout the country.

That is a pity because, whatever its motivation, it amounts to a psychological assault on most Australians. Because it is not accompanied by an acknowledgment of national origins the ceremony ritually degrades most Australians' sense of national identity and alienates the nation from its homeland and from most of its history.

The saddest examples are recitations at school assemblies, where children are told, repeatedly throughout the year, that their country belongs to Aborigines and Torres Strait Islanders. The Acknowledgment appears to have taken the place of the loyalty pledge. Usually words other than "owned" are used, but the meaning is clear. One school I have observed concludes its ritual with the words "under the concrete and asphalt, this land was, is, and always shall be, the traditional lands of [the local indigenous people]". The ritual makes no reference to the ancestors or national identity of the overwhelming majority of students – only 3 per cent of Australians are of indigenous descent. The Acknowledgment is a ritualised slap in the face to most Australians.

We all need secure communal identities that position us historically, culturally and geographically. That is especially true of children and young adults. The Acknowledgment of Country ritual is meant to affirm that identity and pride for indigenous peoples. But it ignores the origins of the nation as a whole. The Aboriginal acknowledgment is justified as a statement of origins. But national origins consist of much more than indigenous prior habitation. The AoC needs to be supplemented to become an Acknowledgment of Nation (AoN), one that accurately describes national origins.

Any recitation of national origins should have at its heart a historically accurate description of how the nation was founded. Indigenous Australians are a part of that story because their ancestors occupied the land when it was settled under British auspices. Aborigines and Torres Strait Islanders are Australia's first peoples. Anglo Australians are Australia's first nation.

An acknowledgment of the historic nation needs to talk primarily about the people among whom national consciousness first arose in the late nineteenth century. Who were they and who did they think they were? The acknowledgment should also state the connection between this national awakening and the establishment of the

Commonwealth, formed in 1901 when the self-governing colonies became states within the new Federation. It is often asserted that the nation began in 1901 with Federation, but that is not true.

National consciousness arose among people of mostly British descent who thought of themselves as such. At the time there was no Commonwealth but self-governing colonies. Most thought of Britain as the mother country but also identified with Australia. This was the most cohesive class of nation, an ethnic group living in its homeland. It was not the type of "nation" whose only social glue is belief in an ideology or set of values or a constitution. It was the heavy duty type of bond, the kind needed to undertake great things. Indeed, this identification inspired and facilitated the constitutional conventions of the 1890s, with the goal of federating the colonies for the purposes of common defence and economy. The nation created the Commonwealth.

An organising principle of the proposed AoN is that peoples take priority over political systems. The nation has priority of recognition because it was the first nation in Australia and created the Commonwealth. It represents continuity of identity stretching back to the emergence, in the second half of the nineteenth century, of national feeling among people who thought of themselves as a branch of the British people and Empire. That consciousness and descent connected the new nation to the First Fleet of 1788, to Britain and its constituent nations, to Christendom and its European precursors in ancient times. In that sense the Australian nation has roots as ancient as the indigenous peoples it absorbed. In addition the descendants of the historic nation and those who have assimilated into it remain the largest ethnic group in Australia. It is also the leading culture in the sense that all other ethnicities tend to acculturate to it more than vice versa.

The indigenous peoples should be acknowledged because they identified with their parts of Australia long before British colonisation began. Any recognition of origins demands acknowledgment of indigenous peoples, whether one believes that their lands were annexed or conquered by the British.

The Federal Commonwealth should be acknowledged because it is the original instrument of continent-wide government and the institutional basis for citizenship, which defines the rights and duties of all Australians.

A brief statement necessarily fails to acknowledge all contributions to origins, some important. For example, the statement recognises the explorers and pioneers and that they came under British auspices but it does not acknowledge the nations of Britain – England, Wales, Scotland and Ireland. Nor does it acknowledge the investment made by the British people through their government in colonising Australia. The statement does not mention convicts, subsuming them under the category of (involuntary) pioneers. Nor does it mention the contributions of law, politics, culture, national character and technology brought by the largely British settlers. Also unmentioned are the hundreds of indigenous peoples and languages, their way of life and spirituality, and special connection with their lands. It would be appropriate for acknowledgments recited in particular districts to name and describe the local culture, which would convey a greater degree of particularity.

The Christianity of the nation's founders is made explicit in the proposed Acknowledgment because it was a prominent conscious element of their identity, as it was of Britain and the remainder of Western civilisation in Europe and America.

Some will object that the proposed AoN omits the non-Anglo-Celtic identities that now form a substantial fraction of the population. Typically those identities are encompassed using the adjectives "multicultural" and "diverse". It is sometimes contended that Australia is no longer an Anglo nation, that it has become a new type of nation whose identity consists of the multicultural character of its citizens. It is sometimes argued that Australia's lack of a single cultural identity is now its identifying mark. And a likely assertion will be that an acknowledgment that omits the non-Anglo elements of the nation would be divisive by creating ill-feeling among millions of citizens. This potential objection should be taken seriously, though it is noteworthy that those who promote and accept the present acknowledgment ceremony express no concern about its own exclusions.

It is reasonable to reject the objection on two grounds. Firstly, the diversity that has arisen in recent decades was not part of national origins. Recall that the nation emerged by about 1880. It is wrong to claim that diversity was a founding principle then or in 1901. Not diversity but continuity with British and European identity was in the minds of the Founders and in the census statistics. The nation and Commonwealth were in existence long before diversity began rising after the Second World War. Unless the Acknowledgment is to become a running commentary on every demographic change, it should remain focused on origins. If it were to focus on the present population instead of origins, that would necessarily demote the indigenous component. If they alone were given special acknowledgment, that would unfairly demote the historic nation.

The second reason it is unnecessary to acknowledge diversity in a statement of national origins is that the proposed AoN recognises the Commonwealth and citizenship, which encompasses Australians of all backgrounds. It is not beyond the maturity of immigrants or their children to acknowledge that the nation was in existence before they arrived.

If it were decided to acknowledge multicultural Australia, two avenues present themselves. The first would be for the acknowledgment to list all the ethnicities of post WWII immigrants, perhaps on a first-come-first-served basis. The second would be to refer to these peoples collectively as "multicultural". I think that most would reject the first approach as impractical. However, the latter ignores the actual identities of citizens. For example, to include Italian Australians under the heading "multicultural" would give no particular recognition to that culture; the same term would apply if not one Italian had immigrated after 1949. The same term would apply to any diverse country. It seems the only practicable way to recognise the country's diversity would be in terms that are exceedingly shallow.

Placing the historic nation and Commonwealth in the acknowledgment ritual would restore their proper places in the story of Australia. An Acknowledgment of Nation would be relevant to all Australians.

Another acknowledgment: This is the latest in a series of versions posted since late 2014. I thank all those who corresponded with me on the subject for their suggestions.

Chapters 3-5:
The Misguided Case
for Indigenous Recognition
in the Constitution

3. Misguided—Part I: The Muddled Debate over Racial Discrimination[*]

When I first read of the proposal to recognise indigenous Australians in the Constitution, I thought: *it's about time.* Recognition is the honest and empathic thing to do. If I were of indigenous descent, knowing that my country had been colonised and my people reduced from sole occupants to a small and marginalised minority, I would want my people recognised in a form that would build their pride and gain respect from other Australians. In addition the status brought by constitutional recognition would be adaptive in the biological sense of group survival. Aborigines are related genetically to one another like first cousins compared to White Australians[1] and I know that in their position I would have fraternal feelings towards ethnic kin due to shared culture and ancestry.

---

[*] Salter, F. K. (2013). The misguided case for indigenous recognition in the Constitution. Part I: The muddled debate over racial discrimination. *Quadrant, 57*(12), 28-40.

Australia's First Peoples—Aborigines and Torres Strait Islanders—have a claim to recognition in the Constitution second only to Australia's historic nation, the continent-wide community of sentiment and shared culture, memories and homeland that awakened in the second half of the nineteenth century. That nation by now includes many people of indigenous descent and the descendants of immigrants from around the world. Like all ethnic families, indigenous peoples have a vital interest in continuity and status. I understand their wish to place that interest beyond the vagaries of ideological fashion. It is right and reasonable for citizens to pursue their interests when those do not conflict with vital national interests. Like many Australians I respect indigenous aspiration for recognition and fair treatment.

Then I read the recommended changes to the referendum. These are in the *Report* of the Expert Panel appointed by former Prime Minister Julia Gillard. The changes are unacceptable, even if placed in the Constitution's preamble, primarily because they fail to recognise the origins of the Australian nation. The amendments would symbolically, and legally if the panel had their way, alienate the nation from its homeland. This flaw is compounded by poor arguments. Contrary to the panel's advice, constitutional recognition will not close the gap in indigenous health, criminality and employment. The genuine ground for recognising indigenous peoples—that doing so would establish historical truth about the country's origins—also applies to British settlement and the original Anglo nation which gave Australia its name.

The Expert Panel's *Report* [2] is a sinister document. It is biased ideologically and ethnically against the traditional Australian nation. Its analysis is flawed by the same ideological distortions and intolerance that have plagued multiculturalism since its inception. It contains psychological and legal traps which if allowed into the Constitution will be sources of endless demands, litigation and propaganda. Social cohesion would be undermined.

This essay has eight parts. The first summarises the *Report*'s recommendations, showing how they would, if accepted in a referendum, create an ethnic constitution that privileges indigenous peoples, subordinates the Anglo majority, and reduces the government's ability to protect the national interest. The next four parts discuss the *Report*'s irrationality. Part two examines the *Report*'s contentions about Aboriginal disability, the overcoming of which is a leading goal of the recognition movement. The third part discusses the equally confused subject of nationhood, also central to indigenous issues and recognition. Part four describes the panel's reliance on erroneous ideas coming from the United Nations. Part five reviews how cultural Marxist notions of race undermined the *Report*. The latter two parts intersect in the radical anthropologist Ashley Montagu, who was given prominence in the *Report*. Part 6 reviews how Montagu's anti-Western and pro-Soviet ideology became influential in the media and academe. Part seven examines the anti-Anglo bias of the panel's personnel. Finally, Part eight proposes a form of constitutional recognition in which national and indigenous origins might be recognised in appropriate relation to one another. The essay concludes that the *Report*—and by extension any referendum based upon it—should be rejected because it fails to maintain minimum standards of truth and fails to recognise the historic nation.

An ethnically biased constitution

If the Expert Panel's *Report* is a guide, Australia is headed towards an ethnic Constitution, one that establishes in perpetuity special status and rights for indigenous and only indigenous Australians.

The Expert Panel urges five amendments. Two would recognise indigenous peoples; three would prevent the government from discriminating on the basis of race.[3] The first proposed amendment regarding recognition is a new Section 51A, which lays the basis for the Commonwealth to discriminate in favour of indigenous Australians. The recommended wording follows, with the preambular words in italics and the operative words in plain text at the end:

Section 51A Recognition of Aboriginal and Torres Strait Islander peoples

Recognising that the continent and its islands now known as Australia were first occupied by Aboriginal and Torres Strait Islander peoples;

Acknowledging the continuing relationship of Aboriginal and Torres Strait Islander peoples with their traditional lands and waters;

Respecting the continuing cultures, languages and heritage of Aboriginal and Torres Strait Islander peoples;

Acknowledging the need to secure the advancement of Aboriginal and Torres Strait Islander peoples;

the Parliament shall, subject to this Constitution, have power to make laws for the peace, order and good government of the Commonwealth with respect to Aboriginal peoples and Torres Strait Islander peoples.[4]

The new section is recommended for the body of the Constitution, which would make its affirmative discriminatory thrust legally binding on governments. (Calling the four introductory sentences "preambular" does not diminish their relevance for interpreting the final bland sentence when they are included in the body of the document.) The requirement to "secure the advancement" of indigenous peoples would remain in force even if the special need for assistance no longer existed, as is already true for many Aborigines. It would carry symbolic force even if placed in the preamble.

A constitutional assertion that indigenous peoples' ties of land, culture and language are "continuing" would have great significance when juxtaposed with the *Mabo* ruling by the High Court in 1992. The ruling made native title conditional on continuity of the laws and customs that tie a group to the land in question. Assimilation of young indigenous people is ending that continuity, as admitted recently by Aboriginal leaders.[5] A constitutional declaration of continuity would likely widen and extend claims to native title. When someone who calls herself indigenous has ancestors most of whom arrived in recent history from outside Australia, when she has no more relationship to the land than other Australians, and when she has little or no culture, language or heritage that is distinctively indigenous, taxpayers might still be required to subsidise her "advancement". Thus attempts to revive, institutionalise and perpetuate native identity, law and customs are not as innocent as they first appear. They favour the movement to carve an Aboriginal nation out of the Australian nation.

To its credit, the Gillard government balked at the open-ended provision for advancement. It preferred an amendment that allowed for laws that "closed the gap" between indigenous and mainstream Australia, which would lose force once equality had been achieved.[6] However, this is tantamount to bestowing a perpetual privilege because it assumes that equal outcomes are a reliable sign of fair treatment and are achievable in the foreseeable future. The irrationality of this assumption is discussed below in the section headed "The *Report*'s confused analysis".

Yet no recognition or special protection is proposed for the Australian nation, despite that nation having founded the Commonwealth and even while its identity, territorial bonds and folk ways come under growing pressure from multiculturalism fuelled by rising diversity and a hostile intelligentsia. Only the fact that most Australians speak English causes the Expert Panel to let slip a linguistic clue to the ethno-historical roots of the Australian nation.

The second amendment concerns language:

Section 127A Recognition of languages

(1) The national language of the Commonwealth of Australia is English.

(2) The Aboriginal and Torres Strait Islander languages are the original Australian languages, a part of our national heritage.[7]

This seems a relatively harmless amendment, though it carries inaccuracies in terminology. It is generally untrue that indigenous languages are part of the national heritage, which is overwhelmingly of British and European origin. Indigenous languages might be part of the Commonwealth (state) heritage, depending on the point of view adopted, but it would be imprudent to assert either claim in law without considering the legal meaning of the terms "national heritage" and "Commonwealth heritage" and the possible costs to the country, both material and symbolic, of including them in the Constitution.

The recommendation is valid when it recognises that indigenous language came first. Those languages would become part of the national heritage should they become integrated into the national community. But the proposed amendment disrespects the nation by treating English as inferior.

Indigenous languages are given historical priority and are ethnically identified as coming from Aboriginal and Torres Strait Islander peoples, while the status and provenance of the English language are unremarked. As to status, English is not stated to be part of the national heritage. It is not even recognised as the national language, because "national" is used to mean Commonwealth or state. Thus construed, the "national language" is merely the linguistic common currency of an officially multicultural regime.

There is no empowering or restrictive wording that sets out what "recognition" entails. For example, there is no requirement that legal and administrative documents be in English and, as a goal, only in English. The language is not extolled, for example as the language of law, science and government. Neither is the history of Australia's English language stated, that it was brought fully formed to these shores by British settlers and kept as their people's ancient language before it became the national and international *lingua franca*. Without empowerment and historical recognition, calling English the national language is an empty gesture.

Three of the recommended amendments are aimed at preventing legislation that discriminates by ethnicity.

That section 25 be repealed.

That section 51(xxvi) be repealed.

That a new section 116A be inserted, along the following lines:

Section 116A Prohibition of Racial Discrimination

(1) The Commonwealth, a State or a Territory shall not discriminate on the grounds of race, colour or ethnic or national origin.

(2) Subsection (1) does not preclude the making of laws or measures for the purpose of overcoming disadvantage, ameliorating the effects of past discrimination, or protecting the cultures, languages or heritage of any group.

The media have repeatedly called sections 25 and 51(xxvi) "racist clauses", perhaps prompted by the Expert Panel's claim that Australians "are increasingly aware of the blemish on our nationhood caused by ... section 25 and the 'race power' in section 51(xxvi)".[8] In fact section 25 was designed to "penalise ... those states where Aboriginal people had not been given the right to vote".[9] Thus it was in reality an *anti*-racist section. Its elimination is not high principle but a matter of housekeeping, removing protection of indigenous people that became redundant when all the states emulated long practice in New South Wales, Victoria and South Australia of granting indigenous suffrage. Neither is section 51(xxvi) racist or a blemish, but a necessary legislative power of any society that wishes to retain essential instruments for managing ethnic affairs, as argued below. That section states:

> **51.** The Parliament shall, subject to this Constitution, have power to make laws for the peace, order, and good government of the Commonwealth with respect to:–
>
> ... (xxvi) The people of any race for whom it is deemed necessary to make special laws

The Expert Panel objected to this provision on the ground that it could be used to discriminate against individuals on the basis of race. They considered this so objectionable that they recommended not only its removal but the insertion of the new section 116A, quoted above, that forbids laws or measures that discriminate on the grounds of race or colour or ethnic or national origin but does allow government to discriminate affirmatively for any group it designates as disadvantaged.

The Labor government of the time, headed by Julia Gillard, did not object to the proposed section 116A except for doubting its chance of being passed at referendum. The opposition leader then, now Prime Minister, Tony Abbott, was critical of the substance because it resembled a "single-issue bill of rights", alluding to the long-running debate on that subject. "In examining the report we will be looking closely at the potential legal ramifications of any specific anti-discrimination power."[10]

When we do look closely, the ramifications take the form of legal traps that would impede responsible government. Let us begin with external affairs, which includes immigration policy. The proposed section 116A does not exempt foreign affairs from its anti-discrimination provision. It is likely that a constitutional ban on racial discrimination would result in legal challenges that could tie the hands of governments attempting to stop illegal immigration. From the *Tampa* incident of 2001 some commentators such as Phillip Adams have accused border protection measures of being racially motivated.[11] This is false— far greater numbers of non-whites are accepted as legal immigrants without a public outcry. Nevertheless, the accusation is easily made by a well-resourced human rights industry because the great majority of illegal immigrants are from non-Western countries. True or false, governments in the past could ignore such accusations. A constitutional ban on racial (that is, by race, ethnicity or culture) discrimination would complicate matters. The result is likely to be some compromise of border protection efforts.

A second example is more difficult to separate from race. In 2007 the Howard government reduced the number of refugees accepted from the African region of Sudan due to the high rate of crime they committed in Australia.[12] Was this racist? The government claimed the criterion was geography but the accusation, again, was easily made because the problem population consisted of black Sudanese. The government was accused of rejecting *African* refugees, not those from particular regions.

It is often difficult to untangle geography and culture. Governments might have to choose between appearing discriminatory and sacrificing public security. A constitutional prohibition of racial discrimination such as section 116A would push decisions away from the public interest and towards politically correct cosmetics. According to the Expert Panel, any discrimination that is not affirmative action is totally unacceptable. But what should be the priority of Australian governments, avoiding discrimination (and its appearance) or protecting the public welfare? If the Expert Panel has its way, Australians will be less able to "decide who comes to this country", in John Howard's memorable phrase.

Even if section 116A exempted external affairs, there are domestic situations where ethnically-targeted policies are needed, and not only in the form of affirmative action. The proposed section 116A makes no allowance for national emergencies. In both world wars Australia interned citizens who were thought likely to sympathise with enemy nations (Germany in the First World War, Germany and Japan in the Second). This was clearly discriminatory but cannot be dismissed as improper on that ground alone. Another example is the Howard government's intervention in Aboriginal communities in the Northern Territory. This has been condemned as racist, though its goal was to prevent widespread neglect and abuse of indigenous children. Was it affirmative action to send police and troops into the communities of one ethnic group? That is debatable. Another example is the ABC, which broadcasts a great deal of quality drama, comedy and news from the BBC and other sources in Britain. Is that discriminatory? It is certainly differential treatment. An anti-discrimination clause would allow a legal challenge aimed at making the ABC more like SBS, with balanced programming from around the world. There are many more such legal traps, from mouse-size to kangaroo-size, because discrimination, in the form of differential treatment, is a vital dimension of human societies. I discuss this at greater length in the section headed "UN influence".

The wider difficulty with the anti-discrimination section is that it is open to a variety of interpretations. Many cultures and ethnicities can be interpreted to be in need of special assistance, though the case is harder to make for the majority ethnicity. Thus the proposed section would allow affirmative action for minorities but impede protection of majority interests. The proposed section 116A does not define racial discrimination. Does that term mean differential treatment, the commonsense definition, or the United Nations' very different definition based on reduction of victims' human rights? I also discuss this problem in the section headed "UN influence".

Another general problem is that the proposed section would prevent governments from regulating ethno-cultural diversity, the costs of which I previously described in *Quadrant* (in the June 2010 issue).[13] Diversity promotes a number of social dysfunctions including loss of social capital and an increasing risk of conflict. For that reason ethnic diversity should not be allowed to get too far ahead of the assimilation process. Keeping diversity within bounds is an interest shared by all citizens. Ethno-cultural diversity also threatens national identity which is vested in the majority into which all others assimilate at various rates. The Expert Panel, though staffed by subtle legal brains, failed to mention that 116A would remove the nation's ability to use immigration policy to limit diversity for the peace, order and good government of society or for ensuring national continuity. This double amendment—repealing section 51(xxvi) and installing a new 116A—would disarm the Commonwealth with regard to ethnic affairs. That is the single most deadly trap in the *Report*.

The proposed amendments are outrageous, not because they seek to recognise indigenous peoples in the Constitution but because they would do so without mentioning the nation's British, European and Christian origins, its more than a century and a half of development as a self-consciously Anglo society, and its attachment to the Australian homeland. In addition the proposed anti-"discrimination" section would prevent elected representatives from managing immigration and domestic ethnic affairs to preserve domestic peace and national identity.

The *Report*'s confused analysis

Errors of fact and analysis mar the *Report*.

Aboriginal disability

An argument advanced by the *Report* is that the Constitution's non-recognition of indigenous peoples has caused them to suffer numerous disabilities. There is a well-known "gap" between indigenous and other Australians. The gap includes a life expectancy about ten years less than non-indigenous Australians, "substantially lower" educational outcomes such that 80 per cent of outback Aboriginal children of school age cannot read,[14] a lower rate of employment, and much higher rates of imprisonment and juvenile detention, chronic disease, child abuse and neglect, and family and communal violence. To this could be added catastrophically high rates of alcoholism and neuron-killing petrol sniffing, especially among rural communities.[15]

The argument that recognition would help close the gap is being used to sell the referendum. The *Report* has a featured quote from Timmy Djawa Burarrwanga of the Gumatj clan to the effect that the Constitution's omission of recognition causes lawlessness and anarchy that were previously unknown to

Aborigines.[16] The promise of a cure for indigenous disability is clearly seen as a persuasive argument. The articulate advocate, Aboriginal lawyer and community leader Noel Pearson, sums up the argument with the heading: "Constitutional reform crucial to indigenous wellbeing", discussed below.[17] The argument is being repeated by recognition advocates across the mainstream political spectrum. The argument takes the form of assertion without supporting evidence. "How can [recognition] not help to make inroads in tackling the disadvantage and damage? How can that not help foster more indigenous innovation ...?"[18] The Expert Panel does not offer much more.

The *Report* maintains that the gap will not be eliminated until "remnant discrimination" is removed from the Constitution and "all people are treated equally before the law".[19] Leaving aside the Expert Panel's recommendation that discriminatory clauses be *inserted into* the Constitution; and leaving aside the fact that the panel fails to locate any discrimination against Aborigines in the Constitution (as already amended), let us consider the panel's evidence. Is there any basis for attributing a causal connection between Aboriginal disability and lack of constitutional recognition?

Three submissions to the Expert Panel are cited, from the Royal Australian and New Zealand College of Psychiatry, the Western Australian Centre for Health Promotion Research, and the Lowitja Institute.[20] The first two submissions provide no evidence (the third is discussed presently). Instead they assert, as does the Expert Panel, that non-recognition causes disability, citing other publications as a substitute for describing the empirical evidence. Looking at those titles indicates that they are not quantitative epidemiological investigations able to identify causes of socio-economic disability.

The College of Psychiatry comes closer to making an empirical argument in claiming that indigenous mental health would benefit from constitutional recognition. This narrow issue is apparently a corollary of a general law: "The lack of acknowledgement of a people's existence in a country's constitution has a major impact on their sense of identity, value within the community and perpetuates discrimination and prejudice which further erodes the hope of indigenous people."[21] The law is meant to explain mental health issues, which are only part of indigenous disability. Not explained is how a sense of identity affects overall medical, educational and work status. The law manifestly does not apply to all the other ethnic groups not mentioned in the Constitution, beginning with Anglo Australians and the dozens of ethnic communities that migrated to Australia from the 1950s, most of which have somehow thrived despite lack of constitutional acknowledgment. Neither does it apply to the countries of Western Europe, whose constitutions generally do not recognise the indigenous inhabitants, their ancient history and prehistory. The law is meant to apply solely to indigenous Australians, with the majority of ethnic groups in the world being exceptions.

In a newspaper article Noel Pearson, member of the Expert Panel and leading Aboriginal advocate, argued that lack of recognition in the Constitution hurts indigenous peoples in two ways. First, it produces "existential angst" about the place of their culture and identity in Australia. This, Pearson thinks, takes away the confidence needed to balance assimilation and pride. No evidence or references for this argument, qualitative or quantitative, are provided. Neither are comparisons provided, for example with immigrant communities facing the loss of identity through assimilation or the many Anglo-Australian communities in Sydney and Melbourne who have become minorities and suffer discrimination. The second cause of hurt, Pearson writes, is the Constitution's reference to indigenous peoples in racial terms. Again, no evidence is produced. The one empirical claim is that the race concept is "false", though again without evidence or references to evidence. The same argument is made in the Expert Panel's *Report*. To back its claim the panel cites someone it takes to be an authority, who I discuss below in the section on race.

Pearson's views on indigenous governance are widely respected and contrast with his utopian statements about constitutional reform. His management of the Cape York Peninsula community has produced substantial improvements in indigenous education. Shortly before the federal election of 2013, Pearson joined other Aboriginal leaders to call for the establishment of a Commonwealth statutory body that would function as a productivity commission for indigenous affairs. Regional pooling of resources would reduce duplication and increase efficiency. Pearson argues that Aborigines should be given more responsibility, allowing them to escape the clutches of the white Aboriginal industry, the "octopus of government tentacles". "We are trying to replace an indigenous passivity paradigm with an indigenous responsibility paradigm." This self-help approach is closer to classical liberal philosophy than the proposed constitutional changes.[22]

Finally, a quote from the submission by the Lowitja Institute indicates an evidence-based argument. "The experiences of other countries, in particular New Zealand and the United States, have shown that recognition of a country's indigenous population in its constitution ... provides a basis for good governance and stewardship of the health of the indigenous population."[23]

This assertion should be taken seriously because it comes from a peak research body, the National Institute for Aboriginal and Torres Strait Islander Health Research, and therefore can be expected to be a useful source of information on the subject.[24] The *Report* does not summarise the Institute's analysis. However, a relevant 2011 Lowitja discussion paper is available from the Institute's website. The paper was written by legal scholar Genevieve Howse at La Trobe University.[25] At last the paper trail leads to an evidence-based analysis.

Howse observes that Australia's nine jurisdictions (Commonwealth, states and territories) provide little recognition of the specific needs of indigenous Australians. Where such recognition does exist, there is no provision for indigenous input to the decision-making or implementation process. This means a weak or non-existent legislative structure on which "stewardship and governance" can be founded on an Australia-wide basis.[26] Accountability for indigenous health outcomes is "diffused and muddled". The result is inefficiency, duplication, insufficient funds, and lack of sensitivity in providing equality of access and availability. So far so good.

This plausible argument leads to constitutional recognition which, Howse argues, would reduce administrative confusion, based on New Zealand and US experience.[27] She recommends recognition in the preamble or in the legally-binding body of the Constitution. In the latter case the amendment should state the right of all citizens to health and specifically state that indigenous peoples have special needs. It should also provide a treaty-making power.[28] One benefit of recognition, Howse thinks, would be bringing Australia into line with the UN Declaration on the Rights of Indigenous Peoples (which I discuss below). This would centralise and standardise national policy by constitutionally enforcing special care of indigenous health.[29] Another benefit would be the increased power of indigenous peoples to attract more government health funding. Howse quotes a paper she co-authored that envisages constitutional recognition forming the basis of legal suits to force governments to spend more on indigenous health than they spend on other Australians. This would be justified, the paper argues, by the dire state of indigenous health combined with a constitutional right to equal health outcomes.[30] Also quoted is a paper asserting that indigenous health problems are caused in part by their non-recognition in law. However, in this crucial respect the evidence is not stated.[31]

The theme of money recurs in Howse's paper. She favourably quotes a 2009 report calling for the pooling of all indigenous health funds which should then be used to purchase "the very best health services" that are culturally appropriate and meet indigenous needs.[32] There is no discussion of the biological and behavioural contributions to indigenous ill-health, leaving the assumption that causes always lie outside their communities. This allows the further assumption that a cure is always purchasable with sufficient expenditure. Present aggregate expenditure on indigenous health is not stated and never praised. Budgetary limits do not feature; neither do non-indigenous fiscal interests, a topic that would have to be made explicit if it were not assumed that non-indigenous Australians have an open-ended obligation to provide for indigenous welfare.

The discounting of non-indigenous interests coincides with Howse's criticism of Anglo Australia. She denies the legitimacy of British possession of the continent, the original basis of national sovereignty, and claims that settlement was based on ill-treatment and denial of Aboriginal rights.[33] This judgmental and ahistorical content mars the analysis, as does the approving quote of Paul Keating's demagogic attack on white settlers in his Redfern speech of 1992.

Howse's argument has merit regarding the cost of legislative duplication, the need for culturally appropriate service delivery and for community input. This agrees with Noel Pearson's broader proposal for regional governance.[34] A strong point is her consideration of alternatives to constitutional recognition. She points out that any benefits of constitutional recognition could be gained through concerted government action, an easier and safer alternative to constitutional change. Howse notes that the existing section 51(xxvi) of the Constitution—the one condemned as discriminatory by the Expert Panel—already authorises the Commonwealth to legislate for the special health needs of indigenous peoples. The Commonwealth is already equipped to unify indigenous health legislation in collaboration with state and territory governments.[35] Howse's paper suggests only administrative benefits for constitutional recognition, not direct health or economic ones—and she admits that recognition is not really necessary for either.

The Lowitja Institute's Chairwoman, Pat Anderson, recommended Howse's paper and presented another argument that could be taken as a justification for the proposed constitutional anti-discrimination section.[36] Anderson attributes poor Aboriginal health to "racism". She quotes a survey of Victorian Aborigines that found that 97 per cent reported experiencing racism in the previous year; 70 per cent reported more than eight occurrences. Some of this racism was verbal abuse but much consisted of tone, which could have been due to cultural difference. Respondents complained about ambiguous or unwelcoming behaviour by welfare workers and the assumptions they make about indigenous clients. Anderson explains how racial insults can cause stress, depression and associated maladies.

Does this support Pearson's argument that the Constitution should specifically recognise indigenous people, require their advancement, and ban racial discrimination? This seems excessive given the weakness of the evidence. The claim of frequent insults is overly reliant on self-report and not at all on observation. And it lacks a comparative dimension. Other ethnic groups including Anglo Australians might have complaints about the tone used by welfare officers that would put the Aboriginal experience in perspective. Much of what Anderson calls racism is the universal experience of ethno-cultural diversity, that "monstrous medley of all conditions, tongues, and nations" alluded to by Edmund Burke,[37] which provokes discrimination of all against all, to paraphrase Thomas Hobbes. Should every one of Australia's scores of ethnic groups that experience discrimination be specifically recognised in the Constitution? If so, that document would become a medley of monstrous proportions.

Also, the argument is flawed. Ethnic slurs and slights are experienced by members of many racial and religious groups but no explanation is provided for why only indigenous health suffers from such slights. And indigenous health becomes worse the further indigenous communities live from non-indigenous people and their allegedly discriminatory behaviour, which is the opposite of what one would expect if racism was the root cause. The argument would have benefited from considering biosocial factors.

The *Report*'s assertion of a connection between indigenous disability and lack of constitutional recognition lacks substance. If this is the best case that a panel staffed with and advised by experts can present, it is safe to conclude that constitutional recognition will do nothing to alleviate indigenous disability, unless it results in further land rights and associated rents or an increase in government expenditure. But those pathways to improvement are not asserted in the *Report*, perhaps because they would not be enthusiastically received by landowners, miners and taxpayers. If Aboriginal poverty is caused by factors unrelated to the Constitution, why change it?

What about other causes? The *Report* does admit the existence of other factors, in one sentence.[38] Unfortunately it does not identify and compare those factors, as one would expect in a serious work of impartial analysis. How else to judge the impact of constitutional recognition? Indeed the failure of this important section of the *Report* is egregious; far below the standard expected of a government inquiry.

Perhaps the *Report*'s authors were reluctant to canvass causes of disability, however plausible, that do not indicate the need for constitutional change? Overlooked hypotheses include welfarism, rural location, inadequate schooling, English as a second language and communal decision-making, as argued by an economist, the late Helen Hughes.[39] Noel Pearson mentions such causes but sees them as secondary ("proximate") to constitutional non-recognition, the prime ("ultimate") cause of indigenous mendicancy. As noted, he advances no reason for pointing the causal arrows that way. He even classifies "innate features" of indigenous people as proximate and thus not worthy of consideration. But in evolutionary theory innate features are produced through biological evolution and are therefore closer to ultimate causes than any document, even a constitution.

A characteristic is innate to the extent that it is caused by genes selected in evolutionary history. Population differences in characteristics arise due to divergent evolutionary paths. There has been limited gene flow between Australia and Eurasia for 40,000 years, long enough to result in major biological and behavioural differences.[40] Farming cultures, which began in the Fertile Crescent about 12,000 years ago, have diets rich in carbohydrates and fatty meat, very different from the Neolithic diet Aborigines had until British settlement. The adoption of farming caused the evolution of the gut to accelerate, resulting in changes to the pancreas and other organs.[41] In Europe this lifestyle also brought milk and alcoholic beverages, selection pressures not faced by Aborigines until introduced by white settlement. The resulting genetic differences are plausible ultimate causes contributing to some Aboriginal medical issues, including kidney disease, diabetes and alcoholism.

Evolutionary theories of Aboriginal disability are rejected outright by an Australian social science still crippled by the culture wars of the last century. Not so in medical science. Dr Alan Barclay of the Australian Diabetes Council attributes the early onset of diabetes in Aborigines to an evolutionary history that did not include agriculture.[42] John Boulton, a medical researcher specialising in Aboriginal paediatrics, believes that we need to draw on evolutionary biology to better understand and treat the health disaster that has afflicted outback Aboriginal communities for generations.[43] The proximate causes include poor nourishment of children as well as fetal undernourishment, itself due to mothers consuming alcohol while pregnant, domestic violence and stress. Despite massive medical interventions, twice the proportion of Aboriginal babies are born underweight than non-indigenous babies. This and other factors have cascading impacts on health, leading to babies that fail to thrive who become adults with high rates of kidney failure and diabetes. Boulton attributes a role to epigenetics, in which early stresses are carried to the next generation by alterations in gene expression. Rat experiments indicate that five generations are needed to overcome accumulated epigenetic effects. Other research directed by Jim Penman, a Melbourne historian, implicates epigenetics in cycles of work behaviour and child rearing over the last four millennia. Penman reports rat experiments indicating that epigenetics can affect alcohol consumption.[44]

Work and social behaviour may also have been selected by millennia of agriculture. Farming, especially in societies governed by rule-of-law, appears to select for behaviour promoting goal-directed work and weeds out violent temperaments.[45]

One egregious omission in the *Report* is IQ, which is the single strongest predictor of educational outcomes and is associated with many social and biological indicators. Australian

Aborigines have relatively low IQs by international comparison. Cognitive psychologist Richard Lynn estimates the average IQ of mixed-race Aborigines to be 80 compared with an Australian average of 98.[46] IQ is certainly an innate feature in the sense of being partly inherited. Twin studies indicate that about 75 per cent of the variance in IQ is due to genetic factors. A new technique for measuring heritability, developed with the help of Australian scientists, confirms that estimate, ending a half-century of disputation about heritability of IQ. The new method —called "genome-wide complex trait analysis"—is based not on twins but on hundreds of thousands of DNA markers assayed from unrelated individuals. It yields a heritability of 73 per cent.[47]

IQ is one factor underlying the extraordinary and persistent gulf between white and Aboriginal standards of living. Noel Pearson tries to convey the magnitude of that gulf: "It is as if there is a Third World country in the middle of the First, one showing few signs of development."[48] The situation is worse than that, despite costly assistance programs.[49] Before China embraced capitalism its people were the largest Third World society in the world. Most lived in rural villages subsisting on medieval agriculture. Levels of alcoholism, child abuse and family breakdown were low. The villagers maintained a hard work routine. Economic development was impeded by communist rule despite the population having one of the highest IQs in the world. The proof? When Chinese people emigrate to free societies they flourish in education, business and the professions. Mainland China is rapidly assimilating science, technology and industry at the most sophisticated levels.

The importance of understanding racial differences is illustrated by considering the OECD target of having 40 per cent of young people graduate from university. This benchmark is set by states most of which have high average IQs by global standards. To achieve this for white Australians it will be necessary to set the entrance threshold at the equivalent of an average IQ of about 102.[50] This is a bit low for university studies, according to the American educational psychologist Linda Gottfredson. From this perspective, if policy-makers insist on the 40 per cent target it is likely to result in universities lowering their standards to prevent excessive rates of failure.[51] The situation is worse for Aborigines. For a population with an average IQ of 80 only 7 per cent exceed the 102 IQ threshold. For this population the top 40 per cent of IQs fall above an IQ of 84. Reducing entry standards to this level would still not produce equality of outcomes, because over 80 per cent of whites would then qualify for entry. And of course the situation would not be improved by raising entrance standards, as advocated by some commentators. If the effective entrance IQ to universities were raised to 110, then about 25 per cent of whites would qualify compared to 2.3 per cent of Aborigines.

Australia is not alone in showing poor educational and socio-economic outcomes for its indigenous peoples. White New Zealand students are near the top of OECD educational measures while Maori students rank 28th. Half of Maori students fail to complete high school, compared to one quarter of Anglo and 13 per cent of Chinese New Zealanders.[52] Many factors are involved but the substantial IQ gap, though only half that in Australia, is in the same direction.[53] Maoris suffer many of the same disabilities as Aborigines, though less severely, including a high imprisonment rate, more health problems, more abuse of alcohol and drugs, a shorter life expectancy and greater domestic violence. Contrary to the Expert Panel's expectation for Australian Aborigines, Maoris suffer these disabilities despite having had the Treaty of Waitangi in place since 1840 and gaining special parliamentary representation as early as 1867. It is therefore puzzling that the New Zealand example prompted the Expert Panel's sympathy for a treaty given that alleviating Aboriginal disability is a main goal. There is no evidence that a treaty, or agreement-making power in the Constitution, or parliamentary representation, would have an appreciable effect on indigenous health, imprisonment rates or employment.[54]

IQ alone explains more than half the variation in per capita GDP around the world, a monumental discovery resulting from the collaboration of Richard Lynn and Finnish sociologist Tatu Vanhanen in 2002.[55] Its significance to international relations and the economics of development is compounded by the fact that IQ also correlates with invidious social indicators: unemployment, divorce, children born to single mothers, poverty, incarceration, chronic welfare, and dropping out of school. To these can be added poor health and reduced support by families and communities. Note that these outcomes are not foretold; there are other causes, resulting in substantial variation. Community culture and access to services can make a big difference.

The clustering of behavioural and social indicators is well known among cognitive psychologists. "Intelligence in childhood, as measured by psychometric cognitive tests, is a strong predictor of many important life outcomes, including educational attainment, income, health and lifespan."[56] According to "life history theory", also mainstream in evolutionary psychology, this clustering is due to reproductive strategies that were selected over many generations.[57] The constellation of traits around intelligence, what the late psychologist Arthur Jensen called the "*g* nexus", has been confirmed many times over decades of research.[58]

Much controversy has attended the subject of population differences in intelligence, and understandably so given its implications. Some facts about intelligence should be stated to dispel common misconceptions. First, by intelligence I mean the general factor *g* first identified by psychologist Charles

Spearman in 1904.[59] This is different from specialised forms of intelligence, such as humans' extraordinary ability to process language. These are mental functions most people perform without conscious effort. Another example is empathy, the ability to put ourselves in someone else's place and experience the same pain or joy we think he must be feeling. This social skill is a computational wonder called "theory of mind"; it is not measured by IQ tests. Compared to these subconscious mental abilities, conscious reasoning ability of the kind measured by IQ is effortful and slow.

The second fact is that average group differences do not apply to every member of the group. Belonging to a relatively high g ethnic group does not somehow confer high g on random members. Different populations' IQ distributions—their spreads—overlap much more than they differ. Group differences in g do not cause ethnic solidarity or discrimination. The third fact is that g is not the only cause of academic or life success. Good health, certain personality characteristics, group culture and opportunities to learn are also important.[60]

A fourth fact is that no given level of g is a human right that is somehow inherent to the species. Neither is it an essence that inheres to a particular ethnic group. European-descended populations may have been undergoing a slow decline in the genetic basis of g since the mid-nineteenth century, due to the relaxation of natural selection that usually accompanies industrialisation and government welfare.[61] At the same time industrial societies have shown actual rises in IQ, called the "Flynn effect", named after the New Zealand psychologist who discovered it. Intelligence is not an essence but is labile over centuries. It can rise or fall substantially in a few generations due to natural (or unnatural) selection.

Finally, as up to 55 per cent of the variation in IQ among twelve-year-olds is due to non-genetic factors, one way to improve educational outcomes is to take measures to boost intelligence via nutritional supplements and other interventions.[62] But this approach is not discussed in the media or by governments because of taboos imposed for ideological reasons.

The biosocial factors just reviewed indicate that constitutional change can do nothing to reduce Aboriginal disability that cannot already be achieved by government or informal initiatives. Yet the Expert Panel's case rests heavily on asserting that document's cure-all effect. The real causes of disability are also fatal to utopian visions of racial equality advanced by both sides of politics. Politicians should not be blamed too much for ignorance on the subject, because they have been taught by academics and advised by bureaucrats inspired by unrealistic theories. Even Helen Hughes, an astute economist respected on the conservative side of politics, could raise unrealistic expectations. In her book *Lands of Shame* she explained that only absolutely equal outcomes would allow Australians to prise off their ball-and-chain of moral failure regarding indigenous peoples:

> When Aboriginal and Torres Strait Islander children ... take their places as doctors and scientists, when it is no longer remarked that members of parliament and cabinet ministers are indigenous, and above all when there is no social or economic indicator that shows a lower standard for Aborigines and Torres Strait Islanders, only then will Australia be able to hold up its head because a "fair go" will have become reality.[63]

Hughes was influential because she injected economic rationality into political debates. As journalist Nicolas Rothwell explained in his obituary of her, she helped "transform the map of expectations" for indigenous policy.[64] Politicians such as the newly elected Prime Minister Tony Abbott have also equated equal outcomes with fairness, thankfully mixed with the achievable goal of providing equal opportunities.[65] By setting unattainable goals—in contrast to obtainable and sizeable improvements—academics have helped lock white Australia into the purgatory of self-doubt and nervous spending. The goal of equal outcomes is unfair to Aborigines because it raises expectations that, while achievable for many individuals, are impossible for the population overall for many years to come. It is unfair to taxpayers who would be saddled with paying for remedial courses and interventions in perpetuity instead of building up more realisable programs. And it is unfair to white Australians by implying culpability for Aboriginal poverty no matter how much money they provide or how much they mutilate their Constitution.

Nationhood

The *Report* states that the Constitution is the foundation of the Australian nation.[66] This has been repeated by senior panel members: "the six Australian colonies voted to come together to form a nation".[67] This elementary confusion in terminology and causation is odd coming from a panel that should be expert in ethnic affairs. The causal arrow flies in the reverse direction. The Australian nation existed well before Federation and was a major impetus to the constitutional movement. Asstated by Alfred Deakin, then a Victorian parliamentarian and destined to be Australia's second prime minister, at the Federation Debate in 1890:

> [I]n this country, we are separated only by imaginary lines, and ... we are a people one in blood, race, religion, and aspirations. It is impossible for any man born in or belonging to one colony to pass to the other and to feel that he has gone to a foreign country.[68]

At the same conference Sir John Hall, representing New Zealand, said about the proposed federation:

> The foundation already exists. The foundation exists in that feeling of kinship among Australasians to which so much eloquent allusion has been made. That is the foundation upon which we are preparing to build—upon interests which are common, upon community of race, language, and history.[69]

Australia's leading figures knew the colonies had become a self-consciously Anglo-Celtic ("British") nation, which had formed through convergence of identity and sentiment, not by legal statute. As the conservative writer Peter Coleman observes, by the late nineteenth century Australian nationality "had its laws and traditions, its folk heroes and songs, its Lawsons and Melbas. It created the Commonwealth of Australia".[70] The Constitution is the founding document of the Australian *Commonwealth*, written to create a continental federated state from the regional states that had been established in the period of colonisation and pioneering economic development. Terminological confusion in this area is perhaps due to politicians wishing to retain the word *nation* and the legitimacy it confers. But the fact is that states, nations and ethnic groups are different things.[71] The Expert Panel should have known that.

A different claim about nationhood comes from panel co-chairman Patrick Dodson, the "father of reconciliation". He and his circle of activists maintain that constitutional recognition will help repair relations between indigenous and non-indigenous Australians. Dodson believes it will bring Aborigines into the centre of national identity, so that all Australians can embrace a 40,000-year history in the continent. It would give Australians a fresh start of "fairness, respect and inclusion".[72]

"Reconciliation" is central to both major parties' rhetoric concerning indigenous policy. Julia Gillard, who appointed the

Expert Panel, stated that constitutional recognition is intended to "right an old and grievous wrong" and thus "take us further on the path of reconciliation".[73] This implies that non-recognition of indigenous peoples was wrong, in a constitution that recognises no ethnic group, including the founding Anglo nation. And it implies that recognition will settle old grievances, which is implausible speculation. A more likely effect would be further litigation and jobs in the white Aboriginal industry.

The Prime Minister, Tony Abbott, stated while in opposition that an amendment would "complete our constitution" and thus bring about reconciliation with indigenous Australians. It would achieve this by permanently atoning for our forebears' "hardness of heart"[74] and by reassuring Aborigines that they are not a "historic footnote". It would honour Aborigines for their contribution to the country.[75] The amendment could be a "unifying and liberating moment" beyond any other reform.[76] Abbott lamented the failure 200 or 100 years ago to sign a treaty with Aborigines like the Treaty of Waitangi signed in New Zealand between representatives of the British Crown and Maori chiefs. A revised Constitution would fill the role of such a treaty.[77]

Note how Abbott's position also centres on reconciliation with an even more far-fetched redemptive tone, though as stated earlier this is partly balanced by his criticism of the proposed section 116A that would prohibit governments from discriminating on the basis of race except to benefit selected groups. Still, in Abbott's view an amendment could be a reform to end all reforms; it could unify and liberate all Australians; and cleanse the sins of the fathers. This mirrors Noel Pearson's view that achieving an Aboriginal amendment would transit stages of "crisis, catharsis, renewal".[78]

I suppose allowance should be made for leadership rhetoric as much as for Hegelian dialectics, but it would have helped to have consulted with anthropologists and historians. A genuine treaty could not have been signed with the indigenous people because they lacked chiefs or monarchs to represent them. The Maoris had chiefs, but the Treaty of Waitangi was not a cure-all for conflict with the British settlers because the bloody New Zealand Wars came *after* the treaty was signed. A century later the treaty formed the basis of Maori sovereignty demands.

Reconciliation is an ever-receding mirage because the fundamental problems on the indigenous side are poor socio-economic outcomes juxtaposed with rising national consciousness, neither of which can be resolved by gestures. On the white side the fundamental problem is a cultural and political elite uncomfortable with any expression of distinctly Anglo-Australian national interests or sentiment.

Reconciliation is often used as a code word for white guilt and apology and endless retreat. The *Mabo* decision of the High Court, once hailed as a breakthrough victory for indigenous peoples, soon came under criticism for being too restrictive. Kim Hill, head of the Northern Land Council, recently argued that the burden of proof in establishing traditional title over a piece of land should lie with those who oppose the claim, not with the claimants. Paul Keating has weighed in with support. Hill explains that changing the burden of proof would help claim land that has been subject to "long-term colonisation", in other words where non-indigenous Australians have the greatest investment of resources, community and sentiment.[79] The fact remains that saying sorry in any semaphore will not improve school performance or resistance to diabetes.

Reconciling parties to a dispute usually involves concessions on both sides, but the panel never considered for a moment the possibility that Aborigines and other racial, ethnic and religious minorities in contemporary Australia are under a moral obligation to recognise the Anglo-Australian people as a nation that built their historic homeland through the blood, sweat and tears of their pioneering ancestors.

As for Dodson's idea that non-indigenous Australians will take on Aboriginal history as their own, there are descriptive and prescriptive weaknesses. A nation typically forms around a founding ethnic group.[80] An essential strand in ethnicity is belief in common ancestors. Study after study shows that people generally know where their ancestors came from, many generations after a migration event.[81] Liberal democratic governments have not yet been successful in changing citizens' beliefs about ancestry.

The prescriptive weakness is that government manipulation of identity is unlikely to benefit most citizens. This is suggested by the fact that earlier incarnations of Dodson's proposal were intended to deconstruct the Australian nation. The idea that national identity can be socially engineered by government is standard neo-Marxian theory, pioneered by theorists such as the late Eric Hobsbawm at the London School of Economics.[82] In the Australian case this was advocated by sociologists Stephen Castles and colleagues in their 1992 book *Mistaken Identity*. They argued that advancing indigenous Australians necessitated ending the Australian nation. This would be a noble goal, they wrote, because the nation was essentially racist. At the same time the Aboriginal cause was seen as a truck under which the nation could be thrown. Castles and colleagues argued that national symbols must be continually smashed, using the education system to indoctrinate white children to be ashamed of their ancestors: "Above all, the history of white racism and genocide against the Aborigines must become a central theme of education and public debate, and an accommodation with the Aborigines must be achieved through payment of reparations and Land Rights legislation."[83]

This is not esoteric scribbling but mainstream ideology in multicultural Australia. The idea that justice for indigenous peoples entails humbling Anglo Australia now resonates with anti-national rhetoric on both sides of politics. The changes proposed for the Constitution would not alleviate the condition of indigenous people but would serve a destructive agenda. More promising bases for unity are love of the same land and memories of shared positive experiences on that land. There is no need to assault either identity.

The dramatic concessions to indigenous land rights claims since 1990 are examples of attempts at one-sided reconciliation. Costs to the nation, when discussed, are usually thought to involve only loss of title to or use of land. However, under *Mabo* principles losses to land need not be significant. The greatest potential cost is to sense of homeland. An example is "acknowledgment of country" ceremonies that are common in schools, public meetings and parliaments. These are attempts at reconciliation using symbolic recognition of land rights. Explaining how these could affect cohesion requires a theoretical detour.

Aboriginal land rights movements risk undermining national cohesion due to the importance of a demarcated territory to tribal and national identity. Territorial identification and feeling of group possession are human universals, probably innate.[84] Anthropologist Arthur Keith summarised territorial identification: "[Nations] have a particular affection for their native land ... they would give their lives freely to preserve the integrity of the land and the liberty of its people ... They inhabit a sharply delimited territory and claim to own it."[85]

Native land rights movements typically arise in settler societies such as Australia when previously dominated indigenous peoples find a voice to protest against their dispossession and marginality and ally with other minorities and radicals to win concessions. In all these societies the dominant ethnic group has a relatively delicate sense of homeland, because the collective memories of the new territory are few compared to the rich history accumulated in the old.[86] The Australian nation is young even by New World standards. The first British settlers arrived in North America in 1607, in Australia in 1788. Though a delicate flower, Australia's national attachment to the land is real and heartfelt.

To remain stable and moderate, societies should nurture their core ethnic groups, for the nation formed around them and they provide the strongest glue in the form of common culture, political traditions, and attachment to homeland. This remains true even as immigrants assimilate into the core and in doing so modify it.[87] Continuity is the key and within it territorial identification. A secure sense of homeland anchors the national identity, dampening the need for nationalist rhetoric or external aggression to maintain cohesion.[88] It gives a sense of ownership and obligation that are indispensable in building public altruism.[89]

This puts in a different light the "acknowledgment of country" ceremony performed in schools, public meetings and parliaments. The ceremony "recognises Aboriginal and Torres Strait Islander peoples as the First Australians and custodians of their land. It promotes an awareness of the past and ongoing connection to place of Aboriginal and Torres Strait Islander Australians".[90] As presently performed, the ceremony ignores the nation's identification with and attachment to Australia. As a result, it implies indigenous possession of the territory, which exceeds the *Mabo* granting of access for ritual purposes. The ceremony could not be better designed to make young Australians feel alien in their own country, exacerbating the effect of anti-national school curricula. Should constitutional recognition of indigenous peoples proceed without the nation also being recognised, it will be a permanent legalistic form of the acknowledgment-of-country ceremony.

Such ceremonies should also acknowledge national sovereignty over all of Australia. They should recognise the pioneers and settlers who opened up the land and over time identified with and bonded to their new homeland. The addition of such words would transform the acknowledgment-of-country ceremony from one that severs ties and alienates to one that builds a sense of homeland in all who identify with Australia.

4. Misguided—Part II: Race and the Culture Wars[*]

The Expert Panel's irrationality is compounded by its slavish devotion to the United Nations, an organisation compromised by cultural Marxism from its early days. The *Report* points out that the Whitlam government ratified the UN's International Convention on the Elimination of All Forms of Racial Discrimination (UNCERD) and that signatories are obliged to legislate accordingly.[1] However, it does not report that in signing the Convention, the Whitlam government regretted that it could not criminalise all the acts covered by Article 4(a) of the Convention, such as expressing opinions likely to promote racial discrimination, but undertook to do so "at the first suitable moment".[2] Neither does the *Report* acknowledge the obvious threat this article poses to civil liberties. Although the panel recommended a constitutional prohibition only of government

---

[*]   First published: Salter, F. K. (2014). The misguided case for indigenous recognition in the Constitution. Part II: Race and the culture wars. *Quadrant, 58*(1), 32-40.

discrimination, in its discussion it implied that individual discrimination should be suppressed, again based on the UN: "The Charter of the United Nations ... provides a clear foundation for the international prohibition of racial discrimination."[3] The *Report* respectfully cites several UN documents, including the 2007 Declaration on the Rights of Indigenous Peoples (UNDRIP). The Expert Panel sought out principles it considered authoritative—and sometimes mandatory due to treaty obligations—as guides and spurs to recognising indigenous peoples in the Constitution.

Ideological irrationality has not been properly savoured until one has read UNDRIP, signed by Australia in 2009. The Expert Panel's *Report* was clearly influenced by UNDRIP, referring to it respectfully—never critically—on thirteen pages.[4] UNDRIP was a master document to the *Report*, just as the UNCERD was the master document to Australia's Racial Discrimination Act of 1975.[5] The latter reproduced the UN's absurd definition of discrimination, as discussed below. UNDRIP extends rights to language, culture and land. Its thrust is to build indigenous sovereignty and undermine national sovereignty. Ideological and ethnic agendas make the document awash with contradictions.

UNDRIP declares indigenous rights which entail discrimination on the basis of ethnicity or descent.[6] This runs counter to the spirit of UNCERD, which was meant to eliminate all forms of racial discrimination, though that document does allow for exemptions. Although there is formal protection of state sovereignty (UNDRIP Article 46(1)) and affirmation of the rule of law (Article 46(2)), no countervailing national rights are acknowledged that would limit indigenous demands.

UNDRIP privileges indigenous ethnic solidarity. For example, Article 17(3) disallows discrimination against indigenous individuals regarding labour, employment or salary. But Article 16(1) declares the indigenous right to "establish their own media in their own languages" while enjoying full and equal access to non-indigenous media. This right must involve discrimination in forming organisations along ethnic lines, preferentially employing indigenous people and determining media content.

Article 20 declares the right of indigenous peoples to "maintain and develop their political, economic and social systems or institutions". Article 23 declares the indigenous right to determine their development priorities and to administer their health, housing and other economic and social programs "through their own institutions". These rights mean nothing if they do not allow indigenous discrimination in favour of their own people in employment and associations.

Articles 35 to 37 come close to demanding state sovereignty for indigenous peoples. Article 35 declares the right of "Indigenous peoples ... to determine the responsibilities of individuals to their communities". Authoritative prescription of responsibilities of people is normally a state power. That power cannot be ethnically directed without differential treatment, including excluding people from employment and right of membership. That would seem to constitute racial discrimination as defined by UNCERD. Article 37 goes further in the direction of statehood by entitling indigenous peoples to recognise, observe and enforce treaties and agreements made with states and to have the latter honour those arrangements. The converse of indigenous sovereignty is erosion of existing state sovereignty, primarily that of New World Western societies.

Article 21(2) declares that governments shall "ensure continuing improvement of [indigenous peoples'] economic and social conditions", if necessary using "special measures". Such special treatment entails discrimination—identifying people by ethnicity and making special laws or actions for them. This article resembles the Expert Panel's recommended section 51A for the Australian Constitution (quoted in Part I), that requires governments to advance Aborigines and Torres Strait Islanders in perpetuity.

Other articles of UNDRIP evoke the Aboriginal industry's open-ended ethnocentric goals. Article 26 declares the indigenous right to "lands, territories and resources which they have traditionally owned, occupied or otherwise used or acquired", without reference to the rights or interests of other citizens individually or collectively. Article 27 declares the indigenous right to state recognition of their "laws, traditions, customs and land tenure systems". Article 28 declares the right to restitution or compensation for land that was "confiscated, taken, occupied, used or damaged" without consent.

Like the Australian proposals, the UN Declaration does not limit indigenous rights by time or culture. No mention is made of accepted international laws of possession in past centuries. The declared rights are not limited to peoples recently colonised or who retain their indigenous traditions and attachment to the land. The latter proviso was set down by the High Court in its *Mabo* decision, making Australian legal precedent an obstacle to the UN's radical indigenous claims. Viewed thus, the Expert Panel's recommendations—especially the proposed section 51A's claim about "continuing" indigenous culture, traditions and ties to the land—would circumvent *Mabo* using a legalistic device that removes most restrictions on indigenous sovereignty. This is another trap laid in the *Report*.

The anti-Western thrust of UNDRIP is clear. There were no delegates from Western Europe at the 2013 congress of indigenous peoples, an extraordinary oversight by the UN. It seems the Declaration is not intended to assist Europeans but is aimed at them as the sole perpetrators of colonialism against indigenous peoples. This overlooks millennia of conquest by non-European powers, some quite recent. The absurdity of this bias is illustrated by applying UNDRIP's criteria objectively. Doing so would classify much of the Bantu majority of southern Africa as settlers on roughly equal footing to the Dutch Boers, leaving only the Bushmen and other ancient populations as indigenous.

Similarly Torres Strait Islanders are indigenous only in their ancestral islands. Those who live on the mainland are immigrant communities with less claim to being mainland natives than many Anglo families. The same applies to Aborigines in the absence of a pan-Australian identity. Because the indigenous rights movement presents a united front, non-indigenous people are not generally aware of divisions. But the sentiments of ordinary Aborigines may be more parochial than the overview embraced by indigenous leaders and not at all beholden to the multicultural Left.

Evidence of ethnic divisions within indigenous Australia comes from the experience of conservative Aboriginal leader Bess Price. Price is presently a Country Liberal MP in the Northern Territory parliament and an outspoken critic of domestic violence in Central Australian Aboriginal communities. In 2007 she won the enmity of leftist indigenous intellectuals when she supported the Howard government's intervention in Northern Territory Aboriginal communities, an attempt to curb high levels of child sexual abuse and neglect. One critic was indigenous lawyer Larissa Behrendt, a graduate of Harvard Law School. Another critic was the indigenous support unit at Griffith University in Brisbane, which barred Price from visiting its offices. When Price hit back at Behrendt she alluded to her European appearance and big-city parochialism, consistent with divisions among indigenous Australians. Price called

Behrendt a "white blackfella" who was out of touch with Central Australian Aborigines.[7]

As long as regional identities persist among Aborigines, a Koori is indigenous only in New South Wales and Victoria, a Murri only in southern Queensland, and a Palawah only in Tasmania. Without a pan-Aboriginal identity Palawahs would be foreigners everywhere on the continent, a reasonable designation after 15,000 years' absence.

How did Australia came to sign a declaration as subversive of national interests and common sense as UNDRIP? To its credit the Howard government refused to sign. How did the Rudd Labor government come to approve it in 2009? What led Jenny Macklin, the relevant minister, to state that the declaration set principles nations should aspire to?[8] Did anyone think to strike a balance by proposing a declaration for the rights of nations or majorities?

The UN declarations, UNCERD and UNDRIP, formed the doctrinal background to the Expert Panel's recommendations to alter the Australian Constitution. But neither declaration is in the Western political tradition of consistency of principle and natural justice. Neither do they accord with the Anglo-Saxon tradition of civil liberties, in which freedom to discriminate is an unstated presumption, not an exemption from a general prohibition.[9] The case advanced by the Expert Panel belongs very much in the UN ideological swamp, into which Australia has been sinking for some time. The *Report* approvingly quotes a UN-style recommendation made by the 1988 Constitutional Commission appointed by the Hawke Labor government. The commission recommended that the following be added to the Australian Constitution:

> 124G (1) Everyone has the right to freedom from discrimination on the ground of race, colour, ethnic or

national origin, sex, marital status, or political, religious or ethical belief.

(2) Sub section (1) is not infringed by measures taken to overcome disadvantages arising from race, colour, ethnic or national origin, sex, marital status, or political, religious or ethical belief.[10]

The *Report* did not define "discrimination" in this quote, giving the impression that the term means differential treatment, which captures a great deal of human interaction. In that case the 1988 recommendation would have empowered government to police natural discriminations made by everyone while conferring privileges on classes it designated. The opt-out clause resembles that exemption for affirmative action recommended by the *Report* in section 116A.

The 1988 recommendation and the Expert Panel's approval of it appear extreme in the light of the naturalness and adaptiveness of discriminatory behaviour. Discrimination on the basis of group identity is what humans are evolved to do, and it has become a vital capacity in adjusting to the mass anonymous societies that emerged over the last few centuries. The same applies to segregation, another radical and UN obsession. Segregation due to government-mandated discrimination was rightfully opposed by the civil rights movement, especially in the USA. But that pejorative meaning has become decoupled from those special conditions and is often applied to voluntary arrangements. Overwhelmingly, segregation is natural and morally neutral. People spontaneously are drawn to similar others, whether the criterion be culture, ethnicity, language or religion.[11] In the United States residential segregation by class and race is as pronounced as ever, despite the policing of discrimination.[12] Australians show the same tendency, immigrants often congregating in particular suburbs[13] and school composition indicating some "White flight", though only the latter are singled out for criticism by multiculturalists.[14]

Voluntary segregation is a product of diversity in open societies. John Stuart Mill remarked that freedom means nothing without the ability to choose among whom we live.[15] The philosopher Hannah Arendt took this further when she argued—from a libertarian multicultural perspective—in support of the right of local communities to ethnic segregation in public schools. Arendt, a critic of nationalism, denied any special status for Anglo Americans. Yet she agreed with the US novelist William Faulkner that "enforced integration is no better than enforced segregation". With regard to voluntary segregation, Arendt believed that "without discrimination of some sort, society would simply cease to exist and very important possibilities of free association and group formation would disappear".[16]

Both the UN's convention on indigenous rights and the *Report* by the Expert Panel would have benefited from adopting a more principled universal position. Extra sections could have declared the right of all to discriminate positively, in everyday life, in favour of their people, whether defined by religion, ethnicity, nationality or race. Both should have declared a universal right to free expression of ethnic affiliation and to form associations to advance collective interests.

From the classical liberal perspective there should be a presumption of the right of individuals and small businesses to discriminate in any way they choose. The need to make presumption explicit and binding is growing as society diversifies and multiculturalist lobbies grow stronger and more extreme in their demands. Unrestricted immigration has become a major threat to civil liberties as multicultural states attempt to suppress natural discriminations. As early as the 1970s, Arthur Calwell, the architect of Australia's post-Second World War immigration program, saw the race-relations bureaucracy as a government reaction to the majority ethnic group's attempt to assert itself in a diversifying society.[17] Social control of Western majorities is a prime goal of the anti-discrimination infrastructure. As a result, in many Western societies liberties won through centuries of political evolution are being rapidly constrained as diversity rises.

The only time the Expert Panel departs from the UN is when the UN is reasonable. The 1965 UN Convention against racial discrimination (UNCERD), Article 1 defines racial discrimination more narrowly than the dictionary definition of unequal treatment. Discrimination is unequal treatment on the basis of "race, colour, descent, or national or ethnic origins" that impairs *"human rights and fundamental freedoms"* in public life (my emphasis). So discrimination in the sense of differential treatment is okay so long as no one has his basic rights reduced. As the overwhelming majority of social discriminations do not impact rights basic or otherwise, the UN in effect exonerates most of them. In choice of spouse, friends, neighbours, schools, doctors and business partners, discrimination is normal and unremarkable. (Having special affection for one's own children is also permissible.) The UN allows that racial discrimination is not usually wrong. This is not to suggest that the Convention is normative. An example of its being compromised is the following qualification:

> [D]ifferentiation of treatment will not constitute discrimination if the criteria for such differentiation ... are legitimate ... In seeking to determine whether an action has an effect contrary to the Convention, it will look to see whether that action has an unjustifiable disparate impact upon a group distinguished by race, colour, descent, or national or ethnic origin.[18]

This clause is intended to allow wide discretion in providing special measures ("affirmative action") for designated groups.

The criteria are so imprecise that the discretion in favouring minorities is open to abuse, as multiculturalism and the subsequent UN Declaration on Indigenous Peoples have demonstrated.

The UN definition of discrimination is unstable. The definition construes discrimination to be evil because it violates human rights. But the construct is so abstract and unwieldy that even its own adherents cannot stick to it. They keep drifting back to the neutral meaning of differential treatment, which would be clarifying except that they retain the pejorative content of the rights-based definition. This is the source of much confusion. It is what the Expert Panel did. By omitting the distinctions made by the UN it gives the impression that normal, moral behaviour is questionable. The effect of the oversight is to invalidate much of the *Report*'s claims about discrimination. An example is its pivotal statement that: "The prohibition of racial discrimination is recognised in all the major human rights instruments that have been adopted under the auspices of the United Nations."[19] This is true only in the context of the UN's esoteric definition of discrimination, which as we have seen forbids only those few discriminations that constrict human rights. The panel should have been aware of the UN's definition because it is repeated in Australia's Racial Discrimination Act of 1975, section 9(1). If the Panel had reported this definition, it would have been apparent to careful readers that most occurrences of racial discrimination, in the form of differential treatment, were acceptable to the UN General Assembly in 1965.

Additionally, the UN declarations leave state sovereignty mostly alone, at least formally. States are allowed much rein in discriminating as they wish in regulating interactions between citizens and non-citizens. Again, the Expert Panel broke with the UN where it should not, failing to include an exemption for external affairs and immigration in its proposed section 116A prohibiting racial discrimination. As a result, its recommended anti-discrimination clause would hinder the Commonwealth, for example in selecting immigrants compatible with Australia's needs.

The *Report* is one big booby trap. It also ignores UNCERD where that document forbids special measures that establish separate rights for any race or ethnic group or measures that continue after their objectives have been reached (Article 1(4)). But there is no sunset clause in the Expert Panel's recommended section 51A, which states the need to advance indigenous peoples. Once installed in the Constitution this ethnic privilege could only be removed by referendum.[20]

One place the Expert Panel was misled by the UN, if they needed misleading, was in denying the biological reality of race.

The race concept

The Expert Panel recommended that the word *race* be removed from the Constitution. In support the *Report* claims without qualification that the race concept is "outdated" and scientifically discredited.[21] It devotes several pages to criticising the concept, heavily relying on statements by UNESCO. The UN statements consist of testimonials from selected scientists. Both of the UN declarations discussed above—regarding racial discrimination and the rights of indigenous peoples—deny the existence of race superiority. Actually they show no interest in the fascinating subject of human biodiversity, only matters of superiority and inferiority. It is the politics, not arcane matters of fact, that matter: "any doctrine of superiority based on racial differentiation is scientifically false, morally condemnable, socially unjust and dangerous, and that there is no justification for racial discrimination, in theory or in practice, anywhere".[22] (Notice the chilling assumption that racial superiority, if demonstrated, would help justify violating someone's human rights.)

The *Report*, like the UN statements, presents no arguments or evidence. The case is legalistic and rhetorical, not scientific. It aims at establishing by authority one of the key empirical premises that it uses to argue for the removal of any mention of race from the Constitution.

Space does not permit an exhaustive review of the long-standing debate on race, but suffice it that continental populations of contrasting appearance show multiple biological differences on a scale greater than that seen between races in many other species, such as subspecies of chimpanzees and gorillas.[23] To illustrate the weakness of the Expert Panel's case I shall discuss the first authority cited in the *Report*,[24] anthropologist Ashley Montagu (1905–99). To be discussed are the quote provided by the *Report*[25] and Montagu's most famous book on the subject, *Man's Most Dangerous Myth: The Fallacy of Race*.[26]

The *Report* quotes Montagu's claim that races are not populations "whose physical differences are innately linked with significant differences in mental capacities" reflected in different cultural achievements and IQ tests. This reflects Montagu's long-standing opposition to notions of innate racial superiority. The quote's relevance to recognising indigenous peoples is not explained. In Australia citizens are free to acquire property and vote without passing a test of intelligence or personality. Likewise, families include individuals of diverse talents, yet all are embraced. The Montagu quote is a *non sequitur* where it is placed in the *Report*. An appropriate place would be where alternate theories of indigenous disability were discussed. But there is no such section.

Let us imagine that such a section was included, and that Montagu's statement had been quoted to advance an environmental (non-genetic) theory as a counter to the theory that genes contribute to Aboriginal disability. The statement is too confident to be credible science. Research is not yet conclusive in this highly complex field. The precise causes of individual and group differences have still not been pinned down, though much progress has been made. We do know that races have differed greatly in cultural achievements over the last two millennia[27] and that contemporary populations show differences in intelligence.[28] Populations evolved in Eurasia have made most cultural advances and have the highest IQs. But the causes of such differences remain to be comprehensively explained.

What is the mix of environmental and genetic factors that cause group differences? The scientific debate continues, though the evidence supporting the hereditarian side is strong and growing.[29] This is not generally known because Montagu's radical egalitarianism predominates in the mainstream media and education system as the result of its victory in the cultural cold war. Friendly to or silent in the face of this view are almost all public intellectuals and university professors in the humanities and social sciences. An example is the American evolutionary biologist Jared Diamond, who argues that Eurasia's leading role in developing science and industry had nothing to do with characteristics of its populations but was caused by the continent's benign environment and resources. He contends that Papuans have higher genetic intelligence than Europeans, which has not translated into material culture.[30] The opposite view, genetic determinism with no environmental input, is not advanced by any expert or public intellectual, though it has played a major role as straw man.[31] In the middle are scientists such as the psychologist Richard Lynn, who point to causes in both environment and population, the latter evolved in temperate Eurasia over tens of millennia. This hereditarian theory is a form of interactionism, the generally accepted idea that organisms are the result of genes interacting with their environment. For traits involving many genes such as intelligence, interactionism has been mainstream for a century, while monocausal arguments, whether emphasising genes or environment, are suspect. Extreme ideologies are drawn to singular explanations, whether genetic or cultural/economic determinism. The mass crimes of the twentieth century were committed by regimes that combined singular theories with totalitarian power. Lynn's interactionism looks not only more plausible but benign as well, though his work is ignored by the soft social sciences.

One final note about racial superiority, the *bête noire* of Montagu and the United Nations. A problem for those who oppose notions of racial superiority is that it not only exists but is rather common. That is because group differences are common, and it is difficult to imagine a difference that cannot be seen as an advantage for one side or the other. Another problem for the *bête noire* mindset is that two populations can both be superior to one another. It depends on the characteristics being compared. Another problem is that the pioneers of race science developed methods, such as classification techniques, IQ tests and the like, that do not always award first place to their own peoples. For example, populations derived from North-East Asia generally have higher IQs than those derived from Europe.[32] Such objectivity is beyond the imagination of ideologues.

Montagu's book *Man's Most Dangerous Myth* is perhaps the most famous of many anti-racist publications. The original edition was published in 1942 at the height of the Second World War. I shall discuss just one argument made in a late edition, which comes with the highest academic pedigree. Montagu reports the Marxist geneticist Richard Lewontin's 1972 genetic argument for the irrelevance of race differences.[33] This endlessly repeated argument has had considerable influence. It is used by panel member Marcia Langton, Professor of Australian Indigenous Studies at Melbourne University, and quoted in the *Report*.[34] Lewontin found that only 15 per cent of genetic variation occurs between populations, while 85 per cent occurs between individuals. He, and Montagu, concluded that race has "virtually no genetic or taxonomic significance". Yet physical anthropologists, geneticists and tourists can racially classify races from bones, genes and appearance. The taxonomic dimension of "Lewontin's fallacy" contradicted long-known principles of classification and was formally refuted in 2003 by the Oxford geneticist Anthony Edwards.[35] The argument about genetic significance has also fared poorly. Fifteen per cent variation among populations might seem small but within a population there is only 25 per cent variation among families. Are families also biologically irrelevant? Lewontin thinks so, even rejecting the view that twins resemble one another for genetic reasons. But of course there is family resemblance in a large number of heritable characteristics, just as there is resemblance between members of populations. Our Expert Panel wants to change the Australian Constitution based on such reasoning.

Fifteen per cent variation among populations is substantial for another reason. Recent analysis based on data from the Human Genome Diversity Project shows that ethnic groups are large pools of kinship. Members typically share as many genes as do cousins,[36] making Australian Aborigines a very large ethnic family indeed. Each Aboriginal is a stakeholder in the continuity and welfare of his people. The racial component of ethnic identity is another reason to respect their fellow feeling.

The Expert Panel makes two further claims about race, both dubious. The first is that Australians are coming to reject the concept of race. No survey evidence is presented. Instead, the claim is supported with a quote from panel member Noel Pearson, who claims that racial classification is harmful and "should not matter".[37] This says nothing about public perceptions. Also, it appears to be the naturalistic fallacy in reverse, deriving an "is" from an "ought".

Leaving that aside, is Pearson correct to claim that race is never a legitimate criterion on which to base legislation? That is a broad proposition that goes well beyond the *Report*'s subject of indigenous recognition. Ethnicity is a concept closer to that subject, partly because it deals with self-identity and because many indigenous people are of mixed race. Many Aborigines are of white appearance. As ethnic identity is belief in shared ancestry, someone of mixed descent can feel Aboriginal, and many do. Does it follow that "race" should be removed from the Constitution?

There are two difficulties with Pearson's argument. First, it fails to account for change in the meaning of "race" since 1901. Until the 1930s "race" had a variety of meanings associated with descent groups: a physically distinguishable population; an ethnic group; and a nation. When Theodor Herzl applied the term to the Jewish people in advocating Zionism he meant ethnicity.[38] The latter term entered usage only in the 1930s, and took time to become widely accepted. This means that "race" in the Constitution can be interpreted widely without changing the wording. Differently put, the Constitution does not contain the race concept as presently understood but only the word *race*, which allows several meanings including that of common descent, preferred by the panel. The second difficulty is that the United Nations, from which the *Report* seeks legitimacy, uses the race concept widely. The 1965 Convention against "racial discrimination", to which Australia remains a signatory, uses that term to mean discrimination on the basis of "race, colour, descent, or national or ethnic origin",[39] indicating that as late as the 1960s "race" was still a useful shorthand for a range of descent categories.

Not only can "race" practically remain in the Constitution, it should, because the term as used in that document has broad meaning and because even in the narrow modern sense it is a valid biological and taxonomical concept and is often an important ethnic marker. The Expert Panel, which adopts the cultural Marxist criticism of the race concept, is careful to allow for affirmative action based on racial criteria. The proposed section 116(A) subsection 2 allows for government to discriminate to "overcome [the] disadvantage ... of any group".

In this section I have discussed many examples of irrationality in the *Report*, which falls below the scholarly and scientific standard expected of a government commission. This is reason enough to suspect its proposals.

The *Report*'s failure to recommend any recognition of the historic Australian nation in the Constitution is reminiscent of the national civics curriculum being introduced to schools across the country. This was advanced by the same Labor government that appointed the Expert Panel. Indigenous cultures are a major theme of the curriculum but Australia's British and European heritage is barely mentioned.[40] Both documents are end products of a long process of cultural warfare in the field of ethnic studies.

The culture wars over ethnicity

Much about the century-old culture war over race can be understood by examining the Expert Panel's favourite scientist. Ashley Montagu was a political radical who left his native England for the United States following the crushing of the 1926 General Strike. He became a prolific advocate for radical egalitarianism, arguing for the cultural determination of human behaviour. He criticised theories that linked human behaviour to biology, such as Konrad Lorenz's book *On Aggression* in the 1960s and Edward O. Wilson's book *Sociobiology* in the 1970s. One exception he allowed was his own theory that women are biologically superior to men.[41] Nothing exercised him as much as the concept of race.

Montagu was part of the far-Left school of anthropology founded by Franz Boas. He completed his doctorate under the supervision of Ruth Benedict, herself a student of Boas. The Boasians had captured the institutional high ground of academic anthropology in American universities by the end of the 1930s.[42] The movement's signal achievement was to discredit the theory that population (including race) is an influence on culture. The doctrine spread to other social sciences, promoted by intolerant leftist ideologues such as Montagu. What had been a widely accepted theory became a taboo. The effective promotion of Boas's politically motivated ideas on race helped separate the social sciences from the life sciences. The doctrine's founding document was a 1912 study conducted by Boas in which he claimed that the head shapes of immigrants changed to match those of Anglo Americans. This was not inconsistent for Boas because, although trained as a physical anthropologist, he was a Lamarckian, who accepted that acquired characteristics are passed on genetically to offspring. By 1930 this theory had been rejected by anthropologists, except in the Soviet Union. Boas's data were reanalysed in 2002 and found to yield the opposite conclusion.[43] Montagu favourably cited the head study in *Man's Most Dangerous Myth*.[44]

The taboo on attributing cultural differences to biology is still policed. In 2007 the Nobel laureate James Watson, an early leader of the Human Genome Project and perhaps the most famous and revered living scientist for his co-discovery of the molecular structure of DNA, lost his job for claiming that sub-Saharan Africans have low IQ. He also stated that this would slow their economic development. Both claims are supported by a considerable body of research.[45] The referees of Big Science adopted UN-style intolerance in attacking Watson. For example, an editorial in the peak science journal *Nature* unreservedly condemned Watson's views as "beyond the pale" for making "distasteful" and "crass" remarks.[46] In so doing the journal put tone before truth. Watson himself bent under the pressure and begged forgiveness. He even denied the existence of evidence for his views, despite consistent IQ data from Africa, the Caribbean and Latin America, the United States, Britain, the Netherlands and Israel.[47] As already noted, the evidence for substantial race differences in intelligence is strong, though the causes and prospects for change are not yet fully determined. The cultural establishment's censorious mindset has long been promoted by ideologues such as Montagu, though expert findings do occasionally get through to the public.[48]

Montagu shared Boas's attitude to race and to the Soviet Union. Boas had pro-Soviet credentials, withholding criticism at the height of Stalinist repression.[49] In the first editions of *Man's Most Dangerous Myth* Montagu wrote: "Soviet Russia is the outstanding example of perfect management of ethnic group relations under … unusually difficult economic conditions."[50] This was a decade after the well-known Ukrainian genocide. The Holodomor of 1932–33 took millions of lives and was directed in part at suppressing Ukrainian nationalism. Montagu had still more praise for communism:

> In the Soviet Union a determined stand has been taken against race discrimination. The rational belief in the complete equality of all races has become the official creed, and energetic educational efforts are being made to raise the social and economic conditions of the underprivileged races. Whereas in many parts of the world ruling classes or imperialist governments instigate or refrain from suppressing race conflict for reasons of hegemony or exploitation, communism helps to organize backward races in their struggle for political and economic advancement and liberation.

Montagu also adopted the Frankfurt School critique of the white working class as insufficiently radical: "[communism] contrasts with the attitude of many white labor and socialist groups among whom race interests are stronger than class interests". Resentment of patriotism and anti-communism motivated cultural Marxists to abandon the white working class and promote revolution through immigration, an attempt to elect a new people worthy of socialism.

Man's Most Dangerous Myth impressed Left intellectuals, including Julian Huxley, who wrote a foreword to the 1945 edition. Huxley was also UNESCO's first director-general, doing much to establish that organisation's enduring group culture. Montagu was invited to serve with the organisation to help develop educational programs. As a result, he drafted the UNESCO *Statement on Race* published in 1950, aided by notable social scientists such as Claude Levi-Strauss and E. Franklin Frazier. The Statement was heavily criticised, not least because it emulated the Soviet practice of meddling in scientific debates using political manifestos. Nevertheless, the *Statement* contributed to the 1965 Convention on the Elimination of All Forms of Racial Discrimination, which influenced the Expert Panel's *Report*.

Montagu was politically active, agitating for liberal and humanitarian causes such as principles of child rearing, the rights of native Americans, abortion rights, childbirth methods, animal welfare and humanism.[51] In the 1950s he publicly criticised Senator Joseph McCarthy's campaign to purge communists from the US government. This, combined with his far-Left associations, finally attracted accusations of communist subversion.[52] In 1955 he was forced to retire early from Rutgers University.[53] He was soon brought in from the cold, his career as a public intellectual being aided by frequent invitations to lecture at prestigious universities and appear on popular television programs, including Johnny Carson's and Phil Donahue's.

McCarthyism barely dented Montagu's campaign because it defended a narrow target. We are taught now that the US Senate's House Committee on Un-American Activities was a manifestation of bigotry, when it was something much worse—a final convulsive spasm of the body politic against a threat it barely perceived. The anti-communists fought against Montagu's *ideology* but Montagu, like Boas before him, was also waging a more fundamental battle, against the intellectual defences of Western *peoples*.

Montagu's writing in *Man's Most Dangerous Myth* was rhetorical, interspersed with vilification of the West and tropes borrowed from Marxist ideology. He mixed scientific argument with such claims as that colonialists invented the race concept to justify their theft of native land and that in 1836 "the English were busily exterminating the Tasmanian aborigines". This will be familiar territory to many Australian students.

The culture wars of the time pitted Boasian anthropology against the older, biologically-based discipline of physical anthropology. One of Montagu's many targets was Carleton Coon, a Harvard physical anthropologist whose books on racial classification and evolution contradicted Boasian doctrine of universal equality. Coon's theory—though not his data—was to lose support as new genetic evidence supported the "out of Africa" theory. But it was his data on racial differences that rankled. Coon was seen as representing the conservative Anglo establishment and became a prime target of the intellectual Left. For example, the first issue of the *New York Review of Books* in 1963 carried an attack article aimed at Coon, titled "Anglo-Saxon Attitudes".[54] Montagu was embroiled in the end stages of the academic culture wars over who would occupy the intellectual high ground in the United States. The fight was between representatives of the historic American nation and the new class of radical multiculturalists. In his book *The Rise and Fall of Anglo America*, Eric Kaufmann records how by the

1960s the pro-Anglo forces were isolated and defeated by radicals such as Montagu and his media-connected allies.

Denial of group differences has been a core doctrine of cultural Marxism since the early twentieth century and has been invested in by countless tracts and curricula. It has been highly successful in spreading radical influence. The cohesive movement-like character of this new class—Kaufmann notes its pseudo-ethnic character[55]—helped leftist intellectuals overpower their more individualist conservative opponents. Their influence extended to the UN bureaucracy.

Science long ago caught up with Montagu's and Boas's arguments, though that is not apparent from media reports and university curricula. A major study of the US race–IQ debate in 1988, by Mark Snyderman and Stanley Rothman, found that the mass media had misled the public by giving the impression that science rejects any genetic influence whatsoever. But the researchers could find only one expert out of the scores interviewed who took this view, the Boasian Leon Kamin. The false impression was conveyed by selective reporting of anti-hereditarian opinions from intellectuals not expert in the subject.[56] Ashley Montagu was one of those passionate non-experts reported in the mainstream media. This has also been common practice by the Australian Broadcasting Corporation. A decade later the treatment was given to Herrnstein and Murray's book *The Bell Curve* despite its proposals on IQ, heritability and group differences being mainstream among cognitive psychologists.[57] A recent victim, Jason Richwine, describes how the media have repeatedly enforced the left-liberal taboo on discussion of population differences.[58]

The asymmetry in influence of the opposing sides of the debate over population differences reflects continuing fallout from the West's loss of the cultural cold war regarding ethnicity, fought mostly with domestic radicals. The Expert Panel was a casualty of the resulting irrationality, as reflected in its reliance on Ashley Montagu, an enemy of the West and a well-connected practitioner of agitprop within the social sciences.

5. Misguided—Part III: The Ethnic Bias of the Expert Panel[*]

The makeup of the Expert Panel is consistent with the bias evident in the *Report*'s recommendations, that an ethnically blind Constitution be changed into one that names two relatively small ethnic groups so as to honour and privilege them in perpetuity while omitting recognition of Australia's national origins.

Let us start with the numbers. The Panel had ten indigenous and nine white members. The three ex-officio members were also indigenous.[1] These are shown in the following table.

---

[*]   First published: Salter, F. K. (2014). The misguided case for indigenous recognition in the Constitution. Part III: The ethnic bias of the Expert Panel. *Quadrant, 58*(3), 56-64.

Indigenous	White
Patrick Dodson (Chair)	Mark Leibler (Chair)
Josephine Bourne	Graham Bradley
Timmy Djawa Burarrwanga	Henry Burmester
Megan Davis	Fred Chaney
Lauren Ganley	Glenn Ferguson
Sam Jeffries	Bill Lawson
Marcia Langton	Rob Oakeshott
Alison Page	Janelle Saffin
Noel Pearson	Rachel Siewert
Ken Wyatt	
(Ex-officio:)	
Jody Broun	
Les Malezer	
Mick Gooda	

The Panel seems to have been selected to exclude all but indigenous and white Australians. Racial discrimination is not what progressive governments are meant to do. If accepted, the Panel's recommendations would affect future generations of the entire population, which since the 1970s has become diverse. Where were the Chinese, Vietnamese, Indian and other non-white representatives? Where were the large European immigrant communities—Greeks, Italians, Croats? Apart from co-chairman Mark Leibler, who is Jewish, the multicultural community appears to have been excluded in a Panel of twenty-two (including ex-officio members). This is not to be expected from a prime minister (Julia Gillard) who loudly supported multiculturalism. The then Opposition failed to criticise this affront. Asians make up about 12 per cent of the population, pointing to an unbiased Panel representation of two to three. Did the Gillard government discriminate against them? And did they discrimination against Anglos, who were allocated only half the number of places compared to their proportion of Australian citizens? Indigenous overrepresentation on such a Panel is understandable, but why *twenty-one times* their proportion of the population? If the multicultural orchestra is harmonious, why not trust white and Asian players more? There are plenty of eminent non-Anglos to choose from. Why not trust them? Perhaps they were considered less than sympathetic to indigenous causes? Whatever the cause, the Panel's gross ethnic imbalance undermines its claim to representativeness and fairness.

There were also strong contrasts among Panel members in ethnic loyalty and advocacy. The biographies in the *Report* reveal some striking differences. First, all the indigenous members stated their ethnic identities, while among the whites only Mark Leibler stated his. The other whites appear to be Anglos, though that can only be inferred. Second, all of the non-Anglo members but none of the Anglos declared loyalty to their own ethnic groups. Finally all non-Anglos were activists, "community leaders"[2] for whom ethnic commitment was central to their lives, while none of the Anglos showed evidence of ethnic activism to any degree, except insofar as they worked for indigenous causes. The three ex-officio members were all professional indigenous activists.

The Anglo panel members appear to have been chosen for their commitment to the Aboriginal cause, not as ethnic representatives. A prominent example is Fred Chaney, barrister, once leader of the Liberal Party in the Senate, and recipient of the Order of Australia in part for his services to the Aboriginal community. The connections, expertise and good will of allies such as Chaney have helped forge a powerful Aboriginal lobby.

Chaney also has a history of opposing legitimate Anglo interests, even when they do not conflict with advancing Aborigines. In 1988 he crossed the floor of the Senate to vote for a motion aimed at his Party leader, John Howard. Howard had stated that during times of recession "it would be in our immediate term interest and supportive of social cohesion if [Asian immigration] were slowed down a little, so that the capacity of the community to absorb was greater".[3] The mainstream media attacked Howard's statement for its implication that race or ethnicity are sometimes legitimate considerations in determining immigration policy. Even the Hawke Labor government attacked Howard with moralistic rhetoric along the same lines, though the Labor Party was notorious for playing racial politics. For years Labor had been buying minority ethnic votes with immigration concessions and providing special access to minority lobbyists. The Fitzgerald Report into immigration, published in June 1988, confirmed the widespread impression that the Hawke government had been unduly influenced by ethnic lobbies, allowing them to pull immigration policy away from serving the national interest.[4] Geoffrey Blainey had pointed out at the time that the Hawke government had given the "tiny Asian portion of the Australian population four of every ten migrant places".[5] Ethnic favouritism in the guise of multiculturalism has become entrenched in the Labor Party, with the Liberals entering the bidding.[6] Somehow Labor's racial politics escaped the attention of the professoriate and the media, despite their forensic hunt for Anglo "racism". The 1988 debate over Howard's statement revealed the double standards applied to ethnic affairs.

It was in this climate that Chaney voted against Howard, undermining an attempt just to raise a question about the pace of immigration that was transforming Australian society.[7] He claimed to be motivated by a principled ethical objection to racial discrimination that overrode all other considerations including personal loyalty to a close colleague. Based on his statements at the time, attachment to Anglo Australia did not complicate Chaney's struggle of conscience. By 2010 the principles had changed, and he was able to join an inquiry that included not one Asian, only one non-Anglo European, and not one advocate for Anglos or white Australians. He signed off on a *Report* that recommended constitutional recognition and privilege in perpetuity for only two small ethnic groups, leaving the majority identity unrecognised and undefended.

Anglo or white loyalists were absent from the Panel, a body that dispensed the vital interests of white Australians who make up the majority of the population and the core of the nation. Anglo panelists were influential professionals. They came from various sides of politics. But they all acted as ethnic neuters. They were the types described in Andrew Fraser's book, *The WASP Question*, as members of the one ethnic group that dares not speak or even think its name. But most of the non-Anglo panelists represented their peoples—with unabashed pride and nepotistic devotion.

Anglo Australia was also excluded from the Panel's leadership. The two chairmen were both ethnic advocates. They were Patrick Dodson, a senior Aboriginal activist, and Mark Leibler, an advocate of indigenous rights and a leader of the Australian Jewish community. Dodson has represented Aboriginal interests for decades and has become respected on both sides of politics. In 1989 he served as Commissioner in the Inquiry into Aboriginal Deaths in Custody. From 1991 to 1997 he was the Chairman of the Council for Aboriginal Reconciliation. He is known for advocating "reconciliation". The goal is positive—to improve indigenous Australians' situation by providing them with pride and inclusion in mainstream society. But Dodson overlooks the needs of mainstream society. His is an ethnocentric agenda. The contribution asked of Anglos is to confess their ancestors' alleged guilt in causing indigenous disability and commit to pay until equality is achieved.

Mark Leibler, a tax lawyer by profession, has for many years advocated indigenous empowerment. He also believes that opposition to illegal immigrants arriving by boat appeals to the public's "basest instincts" and risks promoting racism.[8] At the same time he has been deeply committed to the Jewish community and Israel. He has led philanthropic organisations aimed at promoting Jewish settlement and development in Israel.[9] Leibler is well connected at the highest levels of Australian politics and publishes the magazine *Australia/Israel Review*. In its pages he has shown himself capable of tough tactics against those perceived to threaten the Jewish community—which, curiously, included Pauline Hanson, who is not a critic of Jews or Israel.[10] The *Review* is suspicious of opposition to immigration, to boat people, to multiculturalism, and to indigenous rights (in Australia) because it believes such opposition increases the risk of anti-Semitism.[11] That helps explain why Hanson was condemned: the *Review*'s stance is not fully appeased by the absence of anti-Semitism but only by abandonment of policies vital to national continuity. It is difficult to construe this hostile policy as a matter of humanistic universalism because Leibler's website does not feature him criticising Israel's restrictive immigration policy, its deportation of illegal African immigrants or its assistance of Jewish settlements in the occupied territories. Indeed, he is identified with the ethnic-nationalist side of Israeli politics, where the need to maintain an overwhelming Jewish majority is taken for granted.

Dodson and Leibler easily fail to meet the standard of disinterestedness demanded of Anglos, but their ethnocentrism was not sufficient to bias the Panel. A necessary cause was the Gillard government's failure to appoint a chairman or panel members with records of caring for the Australian nation the way minority leaders care for their own peoples. Such appointments would have steered the Panel towards its duty of serving the public good and away from sectional interests.

The Panel's bias helps explain the incongruity of an ostensibly left-leaning body recommending an ethnic constitution. Explanation lies not only in the ideological domain but also in ethnicity. The Anglo members were not at all engaged in defending their tribal interests. Instead they represented political parties, the Commonwealth, Aborigines or universalist values. But the non-Anglo members were typically proud ethnic warriors, motivated to put their peoples' interests first, accustomed to acting on that motivation, and rewarded by their communities and the political elites for doing so. That asymmetry in parochialism has been a key enabler of political multiculturalism from its origins in the 1960s. It justifies a degree of cynicism towards those who adopt hair-trigger anti-racism against the slightest expression of Anglo ethnic preference.

The *Report*'s use of sources was also skewed. The Panel was meant to be composed of experts with professional connections, but little use was made of independent analysts in the social sciences and business. No critics of the Aboriginal industry are cited. None. The Anglo members are all but invisible. The *Report* does make extensive use of quotes by Noel Pearson, Panel member, lawyer, leading Aboriginal advocate, and once protégé of Mark Leibler.[12] Pearson is quoted, often at length, on pages 13, 32, 35, 36, 139, 158, 167, 185 and 211. Pearson's Cape York Institute, which he founded and leads, made a submission that is cited, sometimes at length, on pages 60, 80, 103, 126, 128, 131, 149, 169, 177 and 185. Professor Marcia Langton, a leading Aboriginal rights advocate and board member of Pearson's Institute, is quoted on pages 142, 194 and 200. It is good to see that the Panel included such expertise. However, taken together, the *Report* favoured submissions by indigenous advocates to a degree that did not accord with impartiality or representativeness.

Further evidence of ethnic bias is not hard to come by. Among the *Report*'s recommendations is advice about future consultation. It advises that should the government seek to include new questions in the referendum—questions not recommended by the Panel—it should seek the views of indigenous Australians.[13] In the Panel's view the 98 per cent of the Australians who are not indigenous need not be consulted or represented.

The Report's strange obsession with the race concept was also ethnically influenced. UN doctrine and leftist ideology played their roles but so did Adolf Hitler. Mark Leibler explained in a newspaper comment that his motive for seeking to rid the Constitution of any mention of race was that Nazi race doctrine caused members of his family to be murdered at Auschwitz during the Second World War.[14] Although he praises modern Australia, he believes that "racism casts a shadow here in Australia because it is part of our nation's constitution". As we have seen, this is a false accusation. There is no racism in the

Australian Constitution. His assertion also vilifies the historic nation. It is a grotesque insinuation of a parallel between Australia and Nazi Germany.

Leibler's statement reinforces the need to have had on the Panel champions of the Anglo-Celtic nation. It also reveals misconceptions about ethnicity and ethnic politics. Winston Churchill believed in the race concept. During the Second World War the only power that repudiated that concept was the Soviet Union, Ashley Montagu's model state that had already murdered many millions of its own citizens, brutally suppressed movements of national liberation and after the war began an anti-Semitic purge. Treating Leibler's view as a principle would require *including* "race" in the Constitution, to avoid the possibility of a Lenin, Trotsky or Stalin arising here. It is regrettable that a traumatic reaction to Nazism should motivate criticism of a nation-building constitution that helped defeat that tyranny. More regrettable is the lack of protest from either side of parliament.

Hostility towards Anglo Australia cast shadows within the Expert Panel. Noel Pearson has racially abused white journalists and public servants.[15] Marcia Langton recently responded to a journalist who had sought her apology for defaming him by portraying him racially: "I have been insulted so many times by white Australia that I don't get stressed about it any more."[16] Langton has expressed prejudicial views, criticising "[t]he Anglo preference for supercilious politeness".[17] Pearson and Langton reject the concept of race but cannot help using it to classify opponents. This does not make them evil. But neither are they disinterested. They are erudite champions of their people who they view, rightly or wrongly, as opposed by white Australia. That is normal psychology in competitive ethnic relations. But it disqualifies them from reshaping the constitution of a people they see as antagonistic to their own.

The Expert Panel's ethnic bias was manifest. The government failed to give advocates for Anglo Australia any representation in a panel dominated by passionate ethnic advocates. It is disappointing that when that bias emerged the activist members did not recuse themselves and request a more representative body as a matter of fairness. Instead they accepted a process that effectively excluded the great majority of Australians. That speaks of contempt for Anglo Australia, an attitude tolerated or perhaps shared by the Anglo members, none of whom raised a protest at the relegation of their people. Presumably they were chosen to be ethnically submissive, but one wonders how blatant the hypocrisy must become to incite rebellion. The ethnic bias of the Panel should raise the gravest suspicion about the *Report.*

Principles for recognising national origins

The Dodson-Leibler *Report* should be scrapped and a new inquiry appointed. The new body should be ethnically representative and literate in the relevant social sciences. It should be tasked with recommending changes that would recognise the nation's origins. The guiding spirit should be one of truth and fairness. A statement of origins would include recognition of indigenous peoples as well as the nation's roots in British settlement and the first two centuries of development when the national identity was objectively and subjectively Anglo. If it is right to recognise the first inhabitants, it is imperative to also recognise the founders and builders of the nation, the British colonists who within a few generations called Australia home.

How might the country's British origins and earliest habitation by Aborigines and Torres Strait Islanders be recognised in the Constitution in appropriate relation to one another? First some principles:

1. *Compatibility*. Both the indigenous and Anglo roles in the nation's origins can and should be recognised.

2. *Historical recognition*. Recognition should be limited to recognising the past, even if the country has changed. For example, Christianity played a prominent role in eighteenth and nineteenth century Australia, and should be recognised as part of the nation's origins whatever the present status of that religion. If constitution are to be durable they should record history accurately, not with idealisations or demonisations. Passages about a "continuing" indigenous culture, as recommended by the Expert Panel, are prescriptive and likely to deviate from reality over time. Many indigenous Australians are enculturated to the mainstream. The same criticism would apply to the claim that Australia is the same Christian European society it was in 1901.

3. *Ethnicity*. A fundamental principle is to recognise the ethnic dimension of nationality, not omitting its cultural or racial components. Australia's first inhabitants were not a creed or set of values. Neither were the British settlers. Both were distinctive populations with evolving cultures. To respect Australia's origins is to respect flesh-and-blood communities.

4. *National and temporal precedence*. Indigenous *peoples* deserve to be recognised as the county's first inhabitants. But the first *nation* was established by British Australians in the nineteenth century and it was that emerging nation that brought mostly British technology, religion and political institutions and built the economy. National feeling was a prime mover of the Federation movement that in 1901 established the Commonwealth as its instrument. There is no simple precedence in ties to the land. Indigenous ties were ancient and sacred. White nationhood emerged when Anglo-

Celtic inhabitants began to identify with Australia as their homeland, not sacramentally but with affection, awe and pride. This relationship was local, as it was for indigenous peoples, but also regional and continental, a breadth of identification that was not available at that time or previously to indigenous cultures. Indigenous acquisition of a continent-wide identity has come through their participating in the Australian nation. Thus indigenous ties have temporal precedence, while Anglo ties have national precedence, two compatible statuses to be recognised.

5. *Assertion of continuity.* A matter arises should the historical principle not be followed and the Constitution be amended with words asserting that indigenous peoples have "continuing" cultures, languages, heritage and relationship to the land, as the Expert Panel's *Report* recommends in its proposed section 51A. In that eventuality, fairness dictates that the British and European origins of the Australian nation be given the same prescriptive recognition. Any protection of indigenous culture should also apply to Australia's original Anglo nation. If such recognition is placed in the body of the Constitution, as the Expert Panel recommends, requiring governments to advance indigenous peoples, then the Australian nation should also enjoy legal protection. It should be possible to mount a constitutional legal challenge to government policies that undermine the continuity and majority status of the historic nation.

6. *Civil liberties and the race power.* There is only a tenuous connection between indigenous recognition and the Expert Panel's twin recommendations that the race power be removed and an anti-discrimination section inserted. Both recommendations should be declined (though section 25, which penalises states that do not allow Aborigines to vote, is redundant and should go). The *Report*'s authors realised that affirmative action for indigenous Australians would be

blocked if the race power stated in Section 51(xxvi) (quoted above) were removed and an anti-discrimination clause added (116a[1]). Their work-around is the proposal to insert a special clause allowing legislation that benefits indigenous peoples (116a[2]). That is based on the UN doctrine that positive discrimination is acceptable in the case of disadvantaged groups, which are invariably interpreted to be minorities. This overlooks the fact that in many Western societies the founding populations are suffering from ethnic swamping and political repression as diversity grows. To protect against this threat government needs the power to discriminate in selecting immigrants, using "discriminate" to have the commonsense meaning of differential treatment. The proposed section 116A(1) is defective in part because it bans "discrimination" by government while leaving that term undefined. As a result its meaning is likely to gravitate towards common usage, not the UN's contorted and limited meaning. A ban on government discrimination, as stated in 116A(1), would prevent the nation from pursuing the country's legitimate interest in maintaining domestic peace and national identity, because these ends depend on discrimination (differential treatment) in selecting migrants. Should an insertion with the meaning of section 116A(1) be made, there should be an exemption that allows government to discriminate in immigration policy.

What do these principles mean for recognising both nation and indigenous peoples? Simple historical recognition in the preamble need only recognise Aboriginal and Torres Strait Islander peoples as the first inhabitants, recognise the nation's British origins, and acknowledge the relationship to the land of both populations in their own ways.

Recognition in the Constitution's preamble would not bind government policy. Should proponents of legally binding recognition hold sway, the stakes rise precipitously and even more care will need to be taken to avoid legal traps. Historical recognition could modify the proposed section 51A, with a preambular section and brief prescriptive ordinance, thus:

Recognition of the Historic Australian Nation and Indigenous Peoples

Recognising that Aboriginal and Torres Strait Islander peoples were Australia's first inhabitants;

Recognising that the continent and its islands now known as Australia are the homeland of the Australian nation and of Aboriginal and Torres Strait Islander peoples;

Recognising the nation's origins and development in British-descended people;

Acknowledging the central place of Christianity in founding the nation;

the Parliament shall, subject to this Constitution, have power to make laws for the peace, order and good government of the Commonwealth with respect to the nation and indigenous peoples.

This form of recognition might also be deemed insufficient and assertions of continuity be demanded, as included in the Expert Panel's recommended section 51A. Taking that path would raise the greatest threat to national status and sovereignty, and matters of precedence and protection would need to be stated in more detail.

Some criticisms and challenges to recognising the historic nation are likely to arise.

Diversity should be recognised. One objection to this proposal will be that Australia has changed. It is no longer of British descent but is diverse. It will be argued that if the Constitution recognises the people's identity, it should reflect the new reality, not an outdated and offensive past. That argument could be embellished by arguing that, as the historic nation is now thoroughly multicultural, it should not be misrepresented as Anglo. The objection has difficulties.

First, regarding terminology. The Australian population is diverse but the nation is still largely Anglo, including all those who have assimilated into that identity group. That is because of the distinction between nation and state. Individuals of any background can belong to the nation, but the process takes time for shared memories and culture to accumulate and common ancestry to form through intermarriage. Joining the state (Commonwealth) is much easier because membership is a legal condition conferred by citizenship. It requires no emotional commitment or even convergence of identity. No wonder that multiculturalism emphasises citizenship and discourages expressions of ethnic nationhood. Yet our multicultural society is a nation mainly to the extent that it nurtures, at its heart, Australia's Anglo-Celtic people.

Second, the argument misses the point about historical recognition, which acknowledges the past, not the present. If present reality is to be a principle for constitutional reform then indigenous Australians have much less right to be recognised than do Anglo-Celts. Australia changed more dramatically from 1788 to 1972 than from 1972 to the early twenty-first century. In the first period the indigenous population fell from 100 per cent of the population to about 2 per cent, while in the second period Anglo Celts stayed in the majority. If the society's identity over its first two centuries is to be ignored, should not all previous ethnic identities be treated similarly? The likely reply, that indigenous people were here first, is not based on present reality and ignores the fact that Anglo Australia came before multicultural Australia. Additionally, the argument concerning ties to the land, discussed earlier, also applies to Anglo Australians in relation to relatively new arrivals, who can take decades to think of Australia as home.

Someone is bound to claim that diversity is the country's distinguishing identity and that it should be recognised in the Constitution. But an index of degree of heterogeneity does not identify any society in a meaningful way. The only types of diversity that are recognisably Australian are those flavoured with the historic Australian identity, and it is that identity that belongs in a recognition of origins, not recently acquired changes.

No to sectarian constitutions! Another likely criticism of national recognition is that it would change a secular Constitution to a sectarian one. Some will contend that ethnic constitutions are retrograde and unacceptable in the modern world of diverse societies. Furthermore, Australia would be isolated, a pariah, especially among Western democracies. Andrew Bolt adopts some of these criticisms of the Expert Panel's *Report*, arguing that any recognition of "race" in the Constitution would be divisive.[18]

As Bolt illustrates, these objections also apply to the Expert Panel's recommendations, a point not admitted by supporters of indigenous recognition. The Greens Party, the most left-wing of the four main political parties, approved all the Panel's proposals[19] but is unlikely to be sympathetic towards recognising Anglo history. However, if the Constitution would be unacceptably ethnocentric by recognising the nation's British origins, what makes recognition of the first inhabitants acceptable? Both sides of politics have already agreed to make the Constitution an ethnocentric document. If it is to be ethnocentric, how can Anglo Australia be omitted? How can it be just to recognise only one small ethnic grouping and bind government to advance it forever? Anyone who accepts this recommendation cannot have a principled objection to ethnic constitutions. Including the historic nation in the Constitution would merely extend the principle to include the majority of citizens, those derived from or identifying with Australia's British origins and original Anglo nationhood. If ethnic constitutions are always deemed to be improper, then no ethnic group should be privileged with constitutional recognition. Retrograde? Ethnically neutral constitutions have flaws of their own. Many Western nations with secular constitutions are undergoing rapid displacement within their ancient homelands without symbolic or legal recourse.

Would Australia become isolated? Not if Israel is a guide. That nation has an ethnic constitution and has long been supported by Australia and the United States. Three Australian ex-prime ministers (Hawke, Howard and Gillard) have accepted the Jerusalem Prize for their efforts to forge closer ties with Israel.[20] Serving prime ministers have also seen fit to accept honours from pro-Israel organisations. These symbolic acts imply acceptance or tolerance of Israel's understandable desire to remain a Jewish state. The US establishment agrees.

In March 2013 President Barack Obama, like many presidents before him, affirmed American support for Israel's remaining a Jewish state, and expressed this in the principle of ethnic nationalism: "the dream of true freedom finally found its full expression in the Zionist idea—to be a free people in your homeland".[21] Israel's dream has been built using restrictive immigration measures that Australia's founding fathers would have appreciated, though the White Australian policy was a broad tent compared to Israel's emphasis on genealogy.[22] Obama's ethno-nationalist credentials are considerable, his post-Harvard career being that of a community organiser for the black community. He has repeatedly expressed a special affection for his own people, one that was reciprocated in the last two presidential elections. Republicans have never criticised Obama's ethnic loyalties and, although less overt, play the ethnic game themselves. They receive the overwhelming majority of their votes from whites. The US is Australia's most important ally, so it is comforting to know that national recognition in the Constitution need not upset our indispensable ally.

Academic politics. The ignorance of intellectuals concerning human nature could raise hurdles in putting together a commission able to deliberate on national recognition. The Anglo-Irish political philosopher Edmund Burke observed in his reflections on the French Revolution that the construction of workable constitutions depends on a deep understanding human nature:

> the constitution of a state, and the due distribution of its powers, [are] a matter of the most delicate and complicated skill. It requires a deep knowledge of human nature and human necessities, and of the things which facilitate or obstruct the various ends which are to be pursued by the mechanism of civil institutions. The science of constructing a commonwealth, or renovating it, or reforming it, is, like every other experimental science, not to be taught a priori ... The nature of man is intricate; the objects of society are of the greatest possible complexity; and therefore no simple disposition or direction of power can be suitable either to man's nature, or to the quality of his affairs.[23]

The war on human nature that first broke the surface in the 1960s has diminished the universities as a source of political wisdom. This provides something of an excuse to politicians and the expert panels they appoint. They cannot be blamed completely for fumbling ethnic policy, because they are inevitably influenced by ideas and advice emanating from the universities. I described the corruption of the social sciences by utopian radicalism in earlier *Quadrant* articles.[24] The fallout also affects many conservative scholars, though it is easier to find examples on the Left.

A related phenomenon is shoddy scholarship, whose errors so often favour a radical agenda. An example is some historians' contention that the British annexation of Australia was based on the legal fiction that the country was unoccupied and not possessed, the doctrine of *terra nullius*, a theory with obvious political and legal implications. But James Cook's claim of the Eastern seaboard for Britain was predicated on the land being without sovereignty, that is, not being ruled over by a state. There was no reference to the land being unoccupied or not possessed. The First Fleet arrived with a detachment of marines lugging cannon and muskets. It was forceful annexation, an act of possession recognised at the time in international law. In his book *The invention of* terra nullius: *Historical and legal fictions on the foundation of Australia* (2005) historian Michael Connor describes how the meaning of *terra nullius* has expanded and spread to suit the legal purpose of asserting Aboriginal land rights.[25]

The ideologically driven denial of an innate human nature, the separation of the social from the biological sciences, has allowed utopian intellectual movements to put down deep root in our universities. The indigenous recognition movement derives in part from this radical trend among White academics. How else to explain the sorry reliance of the *Report* on Ashley Montagu's doctrinaire pro-Soviet screed written during the Second World War, ignoring seventy years of advances in human biodiversity research?

This is not an isolated incident. It is telling that Paul Keating's misleading Redfern Speech of December 1992 was received with equanimity by academicians and journalists. The demagoguery was compounded by speaking down to the Aboriginal audience, as if they could not handle an honest assessment of their situation. Two decades later we are still waiting for a statesmanlike corrective.

Overcoming academic ignorance and ethnic bias will involve education. Any movement to oppose the planned referendum and prepare an alternative would benefit from an injection of science into discussions of ethnicity and nationalism.

The referendum process

If a new referendum process is undertaken the cabal of the last Expert Panel should not be repeated, though some of the original members should be invited to participate. A fair and representative process of constitutional reform is essential to ensure a just settlement of ethnic interests. The inclusion of all major stakeholders is a basic principle of democratic ethnic conflict resolution. The responsible government commission should have the substance and appearance of fairness. Realistically, bias and its appearance can *not* be avoided by appointing experts who declare themselves free of ethnic loyalties. The most insidious bias exists below the level of consciousness and besides, ethnic leaders and even politicians have been known to deceive. Around the Western world, majority elites who claim non-partisanship have a track record of acceding to minority demands. It is safe to assume that the Anglos who appointed the Expert Panel and who served in it would blanch at the suggestion that they have any ethnic motives, apart from sympathy for victim groups. Based on their poor performance it would be safer to exclude them and anyone else who claims a post-ethnic orientation. Another reason to include ethnic partisans is that attempting to keep them out would rob an inquiry of many individuals who are best informed about ethnic affairs, including the interests of their own ethnic groups.

The more feasible approach would be to design the Panel as a representative forum that includes leading activists from all stakeholder communities. The forum would allow for adversarial procedure, part of our legal tradition and a fair approach to resolving competing claims. That would be fairer and more effective at winnowing bad ideas. A balance of partisanship would be crucial, and that is the challenge because the present political class considers it unthinkable that the policy process should include Anglo Australians who feel about their people the way Aboriginal and multicultural leaders feel about theirs. Representatives of all major ethnic communities should be included because they, as citizens and taxpayers, will be liable for the costs of constitutional change whether or not their ancestors were involved in the displacement of indigenous peoples. Thus such a panel should include indigenous and minority representatives in a principled and fair manner. Major ethnic groups should be represented in approximate proportion to their share of the general population, except for Aboriginals and Torres Strait Islanders, whose number should be sufficient to form an effective work group and represent different regions. The chair or co-chair of a balanced commission would necessarily have a history of advocating Anglo interests. There would be several other commissioners of like background. Only then would the inquiry conduct – and appear to conduct –its own business instead of being dictated to.

I argued earlier that a representative Expert Panel must include advocates of Anglo Australia. Who would they be? From where would they come? At this point, not one member of the national Parliament has faulted the *Report* for omitting the nation. Academic and journalistic criticism has been muted. As discussed in a previous article, Anglo ethnic organisations are few, a rare example being the British Australian Community based in Melbourne.[26] Any new government inquiry into constitutional recognition of origins should reach out to include loyalist members of the Anglo-Australian community able to contribute to deliberations.

Conclusion

The *Report* on constitutional recognition was written by an Expert Panel dominated by individuals for whom Anglo Australia, the country's majority population and leading identity group, is an embarrassing relic or obstacle to their own ethnic aspirations. This should teach Australians that the cost of ethnic subordination is to be excluded from policy-making forums that dispense status and resources. Anglo Australians lost the cultural war that set the policy boundaries regarding immigration and domestic ethnic arrangements. Being kept out of their own Constitution, having their children indoctrinated at school and having to pay endless rent for permission to live in their own country; that is the price nations pay for not investing in ethnic agencies of the same stature as those arrayed against them.

All patriotic Australians should oppose the planned referendum, which is flawed beyond repair. Unfortunately, elements of the amendments proposed by the Expert Panel have a good chance of passing a referendum because both sides of politics enthusiastically endorse unilateral indigenous recognition, though both parties have selective criticisms. The odds would change dramatically if a major political party took the lead in the NO campaign. At present there is no sign that either side of politics recognises the issue as an existential one for the nation. Should an established political leader fail to step forward, an independent campaign should be mounted. There is time for the stench of the Expert Panel's *Report* to cause a healthy revulsion, at least outside the Canberra beltway. The immorality of the proposed amendments should also work against them. I do believe that most Australians would reject the referendum if they grasped its unfairness in both means and ends. Fair process and democracy have deep roots in the Australian people.

A reason for hope is the healthy instincts of the Australian people regarding national defence. When the Rudd-Gillard government failed to stem the tide of illegal immigrants posing as refugees, one journalist summed up the mood thus: "The Australian people in their overwhelming majority want the national government to reassert national sovereignty over our borders".[27] The public's mood turned despite spin from the ABC and the left intelligentsia. The same sense of outrage and urgency is warranted regarding the proposed constitutional amendments, which if framed in a referendum would represent a fundamental assault on the nation's sovereignty. This time the threat is internal, an attempt psychologically to uproot the nation from its continental homeland and burden future generations with confected ancestral guilt.

If there is to be recognition of our first peoples in the Constitution, there should also be recognition of our first nation.

6. Referendum Traps*

Prime Minister Tony Abbott has stated his intention of holding a referendum to recognise indigenous Australians in the Constitution. The referendum questions have not been announced so it is impossible to praise or criticise their wording. It is appropriate, however, to warn the framers and the public about likely pitfalls, especially when it appears that the Coalition Government is unaware of all the traps awaiting them. Evidence for that is the Government's taking seriously the *Report* of the Expert Panel appointed by the Gillard Government. The Coalition has not accepted the *Report's* recommendations, but neither has it condemned them, more than two years after they were released, despite the *Report* being riddled with traps for good government, social cohesion and national sovereignty.

One snare the Coalition is unlikely to step into is to place recognition in the legally-binding body of the Constitution, as recommended by the *Report*. Indications are that the

---

* Originally published: Salter, F. K. (2014). Six referendum traps. In G. Johns (Ed.), *Recognise what? Arguments to acknowledge Aborigines, but not recognise Aboriginal culture or rights, in the Australian Constitution* (pp. 71-78). Ballarat: Connor Court.

Government prefers the safer location of the Preamble. Also, the Government is unlikely to propose the Orwellian prohibition of 'racial discrimination', also recommend by the Gillard Panel, which Tony Abbott described as a backdoor bill of rights. The proposed section 116A would bar government from discriminating on the basis of ethnicity except for providing special services to disadvantaged populations, such as Aborigines. This would assist the human rights industry obstruct policies intended to manage indigenous affairs, border protection and immigration. Promoting anything like 116A would be such an obvious failure of prudence and such a betrayal of Coalition voters and the citizenry as a whole, that it is unthinkable that parties calling themselves liberal or national would commit such a blunder.

My guess is that the Government will limit reliance on the *Report* to the seemingly innocuous recommendations to recognise indigenous prior habitation in the Preamble, add some other words of acknowledgment, and delete one or more sections from the body of the Constitution. Unfortunately the *Report* formulates these proposals in hazardous ways.

As a result there are six traps in the *Report* awaiting the Government.

TRAP #1: Ethnic bias

The constitutional recognition movement seeks unilateral recognition of indigenous Australians. This would be ethnically biased because it would omit the British pioneers and settlers, their institutional traditions and their Christian religion and folk culture that laid the foundations of the nation. The omission is unprincipled because the reason given for recognition – that it would acknowledge the country's origins – also applies to the pioneers. Omitting or downplaying the British role in founding the Commonwealth would be a gratuitous insult to the great majority of Australians. It is, after all, the *nation's* Constitution. The Australian nation created the Commonwealth to serve its collective needs. In that sense the Constitution belongs to the nation, as its instrument.

The symbolism of excluding the nation from its own Constitution would deal a blow to social cohesion and sovereignty. It would establish, in the founding document, the prejudicial 'Acknowledgment of Country' ceremony that is routinely imposed on school assemblies and other public meetings. That ceremony would be acceptable if it acknowledged the cultural identity of the pioneers and the nation's sovereignty over all of Australia's lands and waters. But in its present form – essentially what is being proposed for the Constitution – it implies that 98 per cent of Australians have an inferior status: that the population apart from Aborigines and Torres Strait Islanders are interlopers, recent arrivals who have not acquired ties or rights to the land.

That would undermine social cohesion because multicultural societies depend on the majority population feeling sufficiently secure in status and belonging that they do not feel threatened by demographic and cultural change. The privileged recognition of indigenous peoples would undermine the majority's sense of security in two ways. First, it would call into doubt the territorial bond that is an essential component of national identity. Second, it would tend to provoke nationalist resentment among white Australians, increasing the risk of polarisation between them, indigenous peoples and immigrant minorities.

In the larger view it would be improper for the Australian Government to call into doubt the nation's sovereignty. And the bedrock of sovereignty is the nation's undivided and unqualified possession of Australian territory, bestowed upon it by the colonising power, Britain, but more fundamentally earned by the sweat and tears of building the nation from a wilderness. Recognising indigenous peoples is consistent with national sovereignty but not if those peoples are attributed a claim to Australia that competes with the nation's possession of it.

Asking voters to approve such a provision would not only lay a trap for the nation. It would also expose the Coalition Government to the humiliation of a no vote, which would be a real possibility if Australians came to realise the injustice of their own Constitution being turned against the memory of those who wrote it. The humiliation and political losses that resulted would be well deserved.

TRAP # 2: Requiring equal outcomes

The *Report* proposes these words for the Constitution: 'Acknowledging the need to secure the advancement of Aboriginal and Torres Strait Islander peoples'. Such words would be dangerous, even if placed in the Preamble. The Gillard government shied away from this open-ended provision and the Abbott Government is unlikely to put these words in the referendum. Equivalent words might be offered, however, such as requiring governments to achieve equal outcomes, to close the gap separating indigenous Australians from the remainder of the population. Tony Abbott has stated his belief in equal outcomes. To demand that outcomes be equalised not only in health and school attendance but also in broad socio-economic measures, would burden Australians with guilt and extra taxes for the foreseeable future.

Pro-recognition advocates claim that recognition would go a long way to closing the gap. The evidence suggests otherwise. According to the Productivity Commission, Australian governments in 2011-2012 spent more than double per person on services for indigenous citizens than on other citizens. An equal outcomes provision in the Constitution would mean that this massive subsidy would be judged insufficient if the gap did not rapidly close.

Recognition will do nothing at all for Aboriginal income or health that does not involve extracting more taxes and other concessions from the rest of the population.

TRAP # 3: Land-grab by circumventing Mabo

The *Report* recommends acknowledging indigenous peoples' 'continuing relationship . . . with their traditional lands and waters' and 'continuing cultures, languages and heritage'. For many, perhaps most, Aborigines, these are false claims. Yet they would possess the authority of the Constitution. It is inevitable that this authority would be used to reinterpret the High Court's Mabo ruling of 1992, which laid down the conditions under which indigenous communities gain land rights. The Mabo ruling made native title conditional on applicants demonstrating continuity of the laws and customs that tie them to the land in question. This has been a thorn in the side of the native title applicants. A constitutional declaration of continuity, even if patently false, would likely widen and intensify claims to native title, and would advance the goal of carving an Aboriginal nation out of the Commonwealth. It would further undermine national legitimacy.

Inspiration for this recommendation came from the 2007 United Nations Declaration on the Rights of Indigenous Peoples, declined by the Howard government but signed by the Rudd Labor government in 2009. This is an ideologically extreme document which, in several places, conflicts with the United Nations Convention on the Elimination of All Forms of Racial Discrimination, to which Australia is also a signatory.

A treaty would be another way to circumvent Mabo. The *Report* did not propose a provision empowering or requiring the

Commonwealth government to treaty with its own citizens. However, Warren Mundine, chief indigenous adviser to the Prime Minister, has urged the Government to negotiate treaties with indigenous groups. This would neutralise the Mabo provisions as assuredly as would asserting continuity of culture and ties to the land. Voters should decline any referendum proposal that advances that agenda.

TRAP # 4: Designating indigenous languages 'national heritage'

The *Report* recommends designating all indigenous languages 'national heritage'. This could have legal, financial and perhaps legitimacy consequences, for example if governments are legally bound to preserve these languages or teachers to instruct school children about them. The lack of a sunset clause means that all indigenous languages would remain privileged no matter how many speakers used them. The wording put to voters should be carefully chosen to avoid liability. The *Report* also recommends designating English as the 'national language', which is insufficient recognition. If native languages with only hundreds, and sometimes dozens, of speakers are officially to be made part of the national heritage, surely English is a much larger and more fundamental part. English should be recognised as the founding national language and protected as the common idiom of the law and government.

TRAP # 5: Change of the race power

The *Report* recommends that section 51(xxvi) be repealed. This section authorises Parliament to legislate with respect to 'The people of any race for whom it is deemed necessary to make special laws.' Repeal of this section would impede governments' ability to direct policies at particular ethnic groups, which they must do in some circumstances, mainly to provide the special needs of indigenous peoples. Most of those uses have been affirmative, that is, the provision of extra services. Unsurprisingly, this has not attracted accusations of discrimination. However, the Howard government's Intervention in the Northern Territory in 2007 was affirmative only with regard to the children it was intended to rescue from neglect and sexual abuse. It was, as it needed to be, a military and police action directed explicitly at Aboriginal communities. To undertake this policy the Howard government exempted the Intervention from the *Racial Discrimination Act 1975*, a manoeuvre that attracted considerable criticism and would have been impossible if the Constitution had prohibited differential treatment of ethnic groups, as proposed in section 116A.

Repealing section 51(xxvi) is touted as removing the race power. In fact the *Report* recommended substituting one race power for another specified in the proposed section 116A. This change would take much discretion out of the hands of Parliament. The new power would favour minorities while the existing provision promotes flexible government, in effect favouring the majority and minorities as need arises.

The repeal is also meant to remove the word 'race' from the Constitution, an explicit recommendation of the Expert Panel, which judged it outdated. To do so without substituting alternatives would spring another trap because it would neuter the Constitution with regard to this important dimension of human identity and biodiversity. 'Race' as used in the Constitution is the term used before the Second World War to designate descent groups larger than the clan: ethnicity, nation and physically distinct populations. This breadth means that the term retains validity when interpreted with an eye to its meaning when the Constitution was written.

The *Report's* case against the existing race power and 'race' was based on a combination of cultural Marxism and ignorance, a disappointing combination in an Australian government commission. It was also due to a pronounced ethnic bias against white Australia and not only in the proportion of Panel members. Most of the minority members had a track record of advocating their ethnic interests but none of the Anglo members did. Ethnic balance in numbers and loyalty might seem a quaint notion in a multicultural society where the majority is routinely excluded from the policy table. But it would have been fair to include majority voices in a high level commission that was deliberating on matters that will impact the ethnic interests of indigenous and non-indigenous Australians alike.

TRAP # 6: No sunset clauses

The special rights recommended by the Gillard Expert Panel – to recognition, advancement, land and language protection – have no expiry dates or conditions. This means that governments would be forced to continue extraordinary levels of support for indigenous Australians, whether or not in need. The Aboriginal industry would become a fixture. Failure to include sunset provisions would violate the provisions of the United Nations Convention on eliminating racial discrimination, to which Australia is a signatory. It would also be dangerous to make expiry conditional on equal outcomes because ethnic groups often differ in preferences and performance even when opportunities are equal.

Conclusion

It is to be hoped that the Abbott Government recognises the yawning traps in the *Report* and the animus or indifference to the Australian people that they bespeak. Any constitutional changes should be proofed against impeding representative government or harming national cohesion or sovereignty. To that end no agenda should be served apart from historical recognition. That would help make the amendments function as a final settlement, the end of the reconciliation process instead of the basis for new demands on national identity, taxpayers and landholders. Above all, if the country's *first inhabitants* are to be recognised, so must its first *nation*.

7. Section 18c, Multiculturalism, and Power*

Andrew Bolt has raised the issue of power in the debate over the government's election promise to repeal section 18C of the Racial Discrimination Act 1975, which he was found to have contravened in a 2011 court case. In his television program, *The Bolt Report* of 23rd March, he asked why the opponents of repeal are so strong. It is an excellent question. Power is a key factor in politics. It would certainly help us understand the debate over section 18C if we knew which groups have greatest influence over government policy. Does Australia have an ethnic hierarchy and if so, who is on top?

Because the repeal of section 18C is hotly contested, the controversy is a natural experiment for testing the influence of the opposed sides. Which are the most powerful voices in setting ethnic policy (domestic ethnic affairs, elements of immigration policy, and indigenous affairs)? Without fierce opposition the repeal would have proceeded with dispatch, because it reflects the opinion of the Prime Minister, his close colleagues and the balance of the parliamentary party and

---

*   Originally published: *Quadrant Online*, 28 March 2014.

because the Coalition has a mandate for repeal due to promises they made during the recent election. Yet the Government's proposed amendments, announced on 25th March, though a significant improvement, represent a climb down from full repeal. The Racial Discrimination Act itself was never challenged despite its illiberal provenance, content and administration.[1]

It remains to be seen how the courts will interpret the changes should they become law. But it is not reassuring that the proposed replacement for 18C would criminalise inciting racial hatred, the sort of fuzzy, endlessly interpretable provision favoured by the multicultural lobby. The proposal also represents a loss for the lobby but not a clear-cut defeat. They will retain the strategic gains made over the last four decades, including a coercive apparatus of legislation, commissions, courts and associated officials and academics developed to suppress white free speech. The lobby's pressure on the Government over recent months caused the latter to vacillate and compromise.[2] The moralistic rage of critics from Labor, the Greens and minority leaders should not obscure their partial victory. They may get more. Hopefully the Government will stand firm but it was on the defensive after releasing the draft legislation. They were successfully portrayed by critics as promoting bigotry.[3] It looks as though the content of 18C will be reduced but survive under a different heading.

18C is being defended predominantly by the multicultural lobby, a coalition of the political left and minority activists. Opponents of repeal include politicians such as the Opposition leader Bill Shorten. Its most energetic and passionate defenders are ethnic activists representing the indigenous, Greek, Jewish, Chinese, Arab, Armenian and Korean communities.[4] The fact that the lobby is leading the charge in favour of section 18C provides a measure of its power and thus a test of theories of political multiculturalism.

Conventional assumptions about multiculturalism do not sit well with the power demonstrated by 18C supporters. Multiculturalists valorise their movement as a noble fight back by victimised "subaltern" ethnic groups against the "dominant" majority. The theory also holds that minority activists are motivated only by equality, social justice and an understandable love of their people, while Anglo loyalists are deemed to be racists or at the least in need of close monitoring. As Al Grassby, the "father of Australian multiculturalism", stated, "[r]acism was introduced to Australia with the arrival of the First Fleet".[5]

The reality, as demonstrated by the fight over section 18C, supports a different view; that the multicultural movement is formidable compared to its opponents, even though the latter represent the great majority of citizens. Analysts such as Katharine Betts, David Brown and Mark Lopez have observed that political multiculturalism is empowered by a coalition between the ideological left, various minority ethnic groups and pragmatic politicians seeking media support, minority votes and donations.

The polarisation evident in the debate over 18C points to ethnicity being a motive on one or both sides. The ethnic activism of the minority pro-18C voices has already been described. The anti-18C voices are largely Anglophones: Janet Albrechtsen, James Allen, Andrew Bolt, Neil Brown QC, Nick Cater, Gary Johns and others.

Are the anti-18C voices ethnically motivated? Their ideological similarity indicates not. If identity politics were at work one would expect them to come from diverse ideological backgrounds, united only by ethnic goals. This is the situation with the pro-18C side, who present an unlikely assemblage of bedfellows: secular politicians and ethnic partisans, Arabs and Jews. It might be argued that the minority components of this coalition is not motivated by ethnocentrism but by a shared victimhood that elevates the importance of ethnic defence. But such an argument, far from denying intense ethnocentrism, explains it.

There is little if any symmetry between the sides in ethnocentrism. The non-Anglo supporters of 18C generally identify publicly with their ethnic communities, are loyal to them and represent them as full or part time activists. Ethnic identity is central to their lives and politics. Those opposed to 18C rarely mention the subject, let alone evince loyalty or join an ethnic support group. They are individualists with weak ethnic identities and no affiliations with ethnic defence agencies. They are suspicious of, if not repelled by, Anglos who show minority levels of ethnic commitment.

The difference between the two sides can be summed up in psychological terms. The advocates of section 18C usually have "explicit ethnicity" (when they are not Anglo universalists), while the opponents of 18C have "implicit ethnicity".

Explicit ethnicity involves adopting ethnic welfare as a conscious goal, leading to purposeful efforts to further that goal. This fits the reaction to Andrew Bolt and section 18C. It seems that because Bolt was perceived as antagonistic to Aborigines he was seen as a threat to all members of the multicultural alliance. The moralistic, harsh and sometimes bizarre criticism of him is typical of the ethnic passions that so often inflame ethnic relations around the world. Bolt was shocked to find himself accused of having views resembling eugenics, the Nuremberg race laws and the Holocaust.

To its supporters section18C has emotional significance because it is the mechanism by which future enemies can be given the Bolt treatment. The section is a valued weapon in the armoury used by the multicultural "discourse police", to use Betts's phrase.[6] That is why Greens spokeswoman Penny Wright saw Government draft legislation to change 18C as "the Andrew Bolt protection bill".[7] Multiculturalism has always been hostile towards Australia core Anglo identity. In practice the movement has been predicated on intolerance and intimidation directed at silencing critics, so it is understandable that minority activists are wedded to section 18C.

Implicit ethnicity is much weaker and diffuse. It does not much engage the conscious mind and can even be opposed by the person's ideology. A person might instinctively associate with fellow ethnics – a human universal – while doing nothing political to defend his ethnic group and even criticising such behaviour as "racist". None of the critics of 18C argue from an explicitly ethnic perspective.

The differences between explicit and implicit ethnicity affect the two sides' relative political influence because explicit ethnicity is a far more powerful motivator than is implicit ethnicity. Highly motivated minorities (religious, ethnic, business) are often more effective lobbyists than much larger but more relaxed majorities.

One advantage of the anti-18C side's low ethnic motivation might be the ability to make coherent arguments. This is the impression given by comparing opposed statements. First some background. An issue central to the debate over 18C is whether it should be legal to hurt someone's feelings on racial grounds. That is because the section states that it is an offence to do something "reasonably likely, in all the circumstances, to offend, insult, humiliate or intimidate another person or a group of people". Andrew Bolt was found in breach of the section because of the tone of his articles. This has incensed free-speech advocates who see 18C as empowering the Commonwealth to police normal social interactions. The debate has stalled at that point because there is no coherent response from the pro-18C advocates. Instead they dwell on the hurt feelings or their own outrage caused by racially offensive language, as if that answers the initial criticism. Perhaps it was this unresponsiveness that led the Attorney-General George Brandis to escalate his rhetoric on 24th March, declaring: "In a free country, people do have rights to say things that other people find insulting or offensive or bigoted." The Prime Minister concurred: "Our freedom and our democracy fundamentally depend upon the right to free speech. Sometimes free speech is something the people who listen to it do not like."[8]

This position attracted non-sequiturs from the Labor opposition. Bill Shorten, the opposition leader, stated that "No one has a right to bigotry, and racism has no place in modern Australia." By omitting "should" Shorten made a simple factual error. Labor Senator Nova Peris, an indigenous Member of Parliament, criticised Brandis: "The Attorney-General's comments are disgusting; they are a green-light to racism and all other sorts of hate speech." A more pertinent response would have told listeners whether Brandis's proposition, which was an empirical one, was true or false.

One can only speculate about the cause of such irrationality. Perhaps it was the speakers' low perception of their audience. Perhaps it was collateral damage from the general decline of education and the politicisation of the universities; or the undeveloped state of public discussion of ethnicity; or terms of abuse such as "racist" also being employed in analysis. It might be due to the influence of ethnic passions, or unholy alliances between secular politicians and ethnic loyalists.

Whatever the cause, rationality does not represent a winning advantage for the anti-18C side because it does not proof politicians against lobbying. In the end, politics is about power, not truth, and an unreasonable viewpoint can hold sway if backed by donations or favourable media coverage. Sadly in modern Australia, political power does not always grow out of logic. Neither does it derive ineluctably from majorities. The explicit ethnocentrism behind multiculturalism has been overpowering implicit Anglo identity politically for forty years or more. It will continue to do so until Anglo Australia becomes a full partner in the multicultural spoils system or, preferably, the multicultural infrastructure – legal, administrative and educational – is dismantled root and branch.

Resistance to repealing section 18C of the Racial Discrimination Act is a measure of the illiberal character of Australia's inverted ethnic hierarchy. Even if the Abbott government manages to repeal section 18C, it will have been a closely run contest.

8. Biased Referendum Questions Crystallise Slowly*

Snails move faster than the bipartisan federal committee tasked with formulating the constitutional changes to be put to the electorate in the planned referendum. The committee is due to submit its report this month (July 2014) but is seeking an extension of time. Indications are that the extra time is unlikely to result in a responsible set of recommendations because the process is befuddled by ignorance and ethnocentric ideology. The country appears headed for a fight over who "owns" the Constitution.

Patricia Karvelas of *The Australian* reports that the committee is bogged down on many issues.[1] Karvelas's report is revealing. (She is likely to be an important source of news about the referendum, having authored many of *The Australian's* reports on the subject.)

So far the committee has rejected the proposal – by the Julia Gillard-appointed Expert Panel – to insert a new section (127A) which would have recognised indigenous languages as the first

---

*   Originally published: www.RecogniseWhat.org.au, 15 July 2014.

spoken on the continent and part of the "national heritage". Also likely to be rejected is the Expert Panel's call for the insertion of a clause prohibiting racial discrimination by any Australian government. That clause was also to contain a special exemption for affirmative action for disadvantaged peoples. However, the committee **is** intent on proposing that the Constitution be stripped of "racial discrimination", meaning especially section 51(xxvi) which empowers the Commonwealth to make laws concerning any ethnic group "for whom it is deemed necessary to make special laws".

Section 51(xxvi) has been called "racist", though the Expert Panel noted in its report that all the special legislation passed since the Second World War to provide special assistance to Aborigines has rested on this race power. The committee would be advised to read that report more carefully, because Karvelas reports that it is now stuck in a legal nightmare of its own imagining. The problem? The committee also wants to allow for special laws to (raise tax revenues to) improve Aboriginal health, employment and education. Without the race power, and without the affirmative action provision, special laws for indigenous peoples could be blocked by a legal challenge against racially discriminatory legislation. The fact is, Aborigines have been benefiting mightily from our "racially discriminatory" Constitution and the Aboriginal lobby wants to keep the good sort of discrimination flowing.

In an earlier article Karvelas reported the committee undecided on whether to include recognition in the preamble or the legally-binding body of the Constitution.[2] In my series of *Quadrant* articles on the subject,[3] I guessed that the Abbott government would refrain from committing such a lopsided racialisation of our founding document. But it appears that even this is being contemplated. (See also Chapter 6.)

Compounding this concern is the continued lack of any hint that the bipartisan committee has cottoned on to the gross bias of the Recognition campaign. The bias consists of the fact that only indigenous peoples are to be recognised as historic, while ignoring the founding people, the British-derived nation that had developed by the late nineteenth century and drove the federation movement that brought together the six colonies to create the modern Australian state. If the goal is truly to recognise Australia's origins, the historic nation must be acknowledged alongside the first peoples.

No wonder the multicultural lobby is firmly behind the Recognise campaign. Both seek to hide the embarrassing identity of Australia's pioneers and historic nation.

Further evidence of ethnic bias is presented by Karvelas. The bipartisan committee appears to contain not one representative of Anglo or white Australians; but it is chaired by the indigenous Coalition MP Ken Wyatt and the deputy chair is Labor MP Nova Peris, also indigenous. Gillard's Expert Panel was similarly undemocratic. Furthermore, the committee is considering the views of indigenous people "across the country", though any changes to the Constitution will affect all Australians who will foot the bill.

It is perhaps convenient that the committee is delayed because the Recognise campaign is skittish about the level of public support. It is easy to lose a referendum in Australia, most attempts having failed. Senator Peris has called for more funds for the Recognise campaign because most Australians have not heard of it. And Tanya Hosch, a director of the Recognise campaign, considers multi-party support for the campaign to be "absolutely crucial" to its success.[4]

The Recognise campaigners are nervous and well they should be. They are conniving in the exclusion of most Australians from the referendum process. If the majority are to pay for recognition, they should be given a stake in formulating the referendum questions. That will necessitate their representatives being given a place on relevant committees, just as individuals with strong indigenous identities and loyalties have been.

9. Shorten attempts to radicalise the referendum*

Bill Shorten has declared that the Labor opposition will only cooperate with the Government to recognise indigenous Australians in the Constitution if a clause banning governments from discriminating on ethnic grounds is placed in the legally-binding body of the document.[1] Also speaking in support of the new policy were Shayne Neumann, Labor's spokesman for indigenous affairs, and Nova Peris, an indigenous Labor senator.

Labor's new policy represents a significant weakening of the Recognise movement's prospects.

If Labor is successful in imposing its view the referendum could repel the electorate. Alternatively, Labor's radicalism could provide the Government with an easy escape route from holding a referendum if public opinion does not firm up in time. And it would provide a plausible culprit. Labor would find itself blamed for the failure of the recognition project.

---

* Originally published: www.RecogniseWhat.org.au, 4 Aug. 2014.

Ironically, in making his impassioned plea for Australia to repudiate discrimination, Shorten supported the report by the Gillard-appointed Expert Panel which was ethnically biased in composition. The panel of 22 had no Asian members; most of the minority panelists but none of the Anglos were ethnic loyalists. In other words, the majority of Australians had no ethnic representation in a commission charged with formulating ethnic policy. Little wonder that its recommendations were biased. Despite the criterion of historical recognition, the explorers and pioneers who laid the nation's foundations are not even mentioned in the Expert Panel's report.

It is also disappointing that the Coalition has not yet rejected the Expert Panel's report but at least it has not embraced the document as has Labor. That distance could prove an asset should the report become radioactive as the public becomes acquainted with it.

10. Greg Craven questions the black armband Recognise campaign[*]

News continues to trickle into the media about a referendum to recognise indigenous Australians in the Constitution. Last week Qantas bought a reckless futures contract by adopting the "R" symbol of the Recognise campaign on its aeroplanes before the wording of the referendum is settled. This should dispel any remaining illusion that Qantas is the "national carrier".

In an all-too-rare media message questioning the referendum Gary Johns explained the "Recognise What?" campaign on the *Bolt Report*. (Saturday 24 August 2014) Johns' new edited book with the same title received a plug. He recommended a simple acknowledgment of prior habitation in a preamble. (He amplified this theme in a recent speech to the Samuel Griffith Society, reported in *The Australian,* 27 Aug. 2014).

Sadly Johns had to explain his position against the headwind of Bolt's view that recognising indigenous Australians would be "racist". It is unfortunate to see this slur, invented by Leon Trotsky, used so promiscuously by an otherwise moderate

---

[*]   Originally published: www.RecogniseWhat.org.au, 27 Aug. 2014.

commentator. Bolt thinks that discrimination is racism, an elementary misconception of cultural Marxism that only reaffirms the depth of left hegemony in much of the West.

Despite Gary Johns' appearance, across the media the trend continued that was set by the Gillard government's Expert Panel – of extreme proposals being thrown up by an alliance of starry-eyed idealists and hard-headed ethnic activists. There is a schizophrenia here. The simple and heartfelt desire to recognise indigenous peoples is mixed with contempt for the nation's history, evident in the Expert Panel's wish to make sweeping changes to one of the world's most successful Constitutions, changes that would restrict representative democracy. Meant to acknowledge cultural history, the changes would exclude mention of the British and other European pioneers and the historic nation.

Bill Shorten has fallen for this black armband version of the Recognise campaign by demanding inclusion of a radical anti-discrimination clause in the body of the Constitution.

Now Greg Craven, Vice-Chancellor of the Australian Catholic University, has injected some realism and responsibility into the discussion. ("Throw off the right number of sandbags and this might fly", *Weekend Australian*, 23-24 August 2014, pp. 17, 21.)

 Craven ridicules the Expert Panel's anti-discrimination and native languages proposals as referendum killers. The proposed section 51A banning racially discriminatory government policy would not recognise indigenous Australians but serve other agendas. Worse, it would . . .

. . . activate vast political controversy. It would threaten everything from policy on asylum-seekers to recently announced security measures [regarding Islamic terrorists].

A similar point was made by Barry Maley, a researcher at the Centre for Independent Studies, in his call to "Abandon change to constitution" (*The Australian*, 5 August 2014). Craven makes further moderate recommendations, such as removing the superfluous Section 25 and minimising the scope for activist judges to misuse new clauses (Gary Johns makes this point too). He notes, plausibly, that for a referendum to succeed, "there must be virtually no respectable, organised opposition" because the electorate is averse to changing its Constitution.

However, Craven misses one major shortcoming of the referendum proposals pointed out by Maley, that they do not balance recognition of indigenous peoples with acknowledgment of national origins; as if national history can be told without giving prominence to British settlement and the rise of a home grown sense of British-Australian nationhood in the late nineteenth century. As Maley noted:

Unacknowledged in [the Expert Panel's report] are those people who created what is "now known as the Australian nation" and Constitution, and their descendants and their culture that turned a harsh continent into a prosperous homeland for 24 million inhabitants.

Craven believes that the Constitution already celebrates British heritage by prescribing Westminster traditions. In fact the Constitution names or describes no ethnic group but would do so in an unbalanced, unfair manner if it recognised only indigenous peoples.

It is this imbalance that renders Craven's final recommendation positively dangerous. He proposes a constitutional amendment authorising parliament to establish a permanent indigenous council tasked with reporting to parliament and cabinet on whether legislation is consistent with an extra-constitutional declaration on Aboriginal empowerment, language and culture. The nation would be omitted from such an arrangement, its own vital interests unstated and unprotected. The Constitution would no longer be ethnically blind. Neither would it be ethnically balanced. Instead it would "establish the Aboriginal people as a favoured class of Australians entitled to pursue advantageous claims not available to others", to use Barry Maley's words.

11. Does reason matter? S18c and the referendum*

Prime Minister Tony Abbott's surrender on section s18c of the Racial Discrimination Act could have far reaching implications for Australia. It was a defeat for reason and principle that may signify a shift in the balance of power within the nation away from liberal democracy and towards ethnic tribalism.

Why did the government compromise basic Liberal values supported by their core constituents? As I described in a Quadrant Online post,[1] the fight over s18c had a distinct ethnic loyalty dimension, though mainly on the pro side. The organised minorities who defended the provision were motivated by ethnic defence, while their leftist allies were accustomed to supporting minorities against the supposedly racist Anglo majority. Both see the Racial Discrimination Act and its administrative machinery as tools for suppressing expression of white ethnic interests, a prerequisite for asymmetric multiculturalism and the replacement-level immigration it legitimises. Critics of the provision were motivated by adherence to the liberal principle of free speech.

---

*   Written: 13 Sept. 2014

Contrary to the rhetoric deployed by the Greens and Labor, the advocates of free speech didn't have an ethnic bone in their bodies, while their clients had little else. The most passionate pro-s18c voices drew on the tribalism that powers multiculturalism, a mass phenomenon that can deliver the support of mobilised minority citizens, including votes at elections; while their opponents, true to the secular liberal Enlightenment tradition, could only appeal to fair play and liberal (including Liberal) traditions.

Most commentators, including James Allan, observed that Abbott's decision was decided by the votes at stake, by political calculation.[2] It was a contest in which one set of debaters was backed by teams of willing voters while the other set seemed unaware that electoral teams matter. As a result millions of potential recruits remained unengaged in the multicultural game. Their potential opinion leaders put faith in reason and wondered why philosophical argument was trampled underfoot by politicians who believe that power is a matter of numbers not truth; who take majority voters for granted but strive to please the smaller but tightly-knit cheer squads whose votes can win or lose seats.

This was a victory for multiculturalism for minorities over free speech for the majority; of explicit ethnic motivation over deracinated liberalism.

And now we have the upcoming debate over constitutional recognition of indigenous peoples. Are we set for the same process, of tribalism triumphing over reason? The weight of argumentation lies firmly on the side of caution. Let me take you back one month to arguments for and against constitutional recognition that appeared in *The Australian*. Symbolically they appeared on the same day that Tony Abbott's s18c retreat was reported.

On left of page was Tanya Hosch, joint campaign director for the lavishly funded Recognise campaign.[3] On right of page was Barry Maley, writing under his own auspices as a sociologist and anthropologist, though it is relevant to note his position as senior fellow with the Centre for Independent Studies, a libertarian think tank.

Tanya Hosch's comment consisted of quoting a number of supporters of constitutional recognition. Some Aboriginal people claimed that recognition was a matter of justice. One stated: "It's important for our identity. It's important to make us feel good, to be proud of who we are and where we come from, and our culture and our people." Another stated that "[w]e need to appreciate where we . . . all come from and we need to [be] mature about what we think of as our true history". Yet another claimed that it would advance fairness. Another asserted that the Aboriginal story should be recorded in the Constitution, because "[o]ur bloodlines are connected to the oldest continuing cultures on the planet". Galarrwuy Yunupingu stated that constitutional recognition would "bring my people in from the cold, . . . bring us into the nation."

Hosch engaged none of the arguments questioning these views, such as the obvious counter that no ethnic group is presently recognised in the Constitution. Instead she appealed to emotion: expectations have been raised among so many and to such heartfelt intensity that failing to "pursue this referendum boldly and with confidence" would needlessly squander goodwill.

There is no indication that Maley's comment was written to oppose Hosch's but it is an effective answer nevertheless.[4] He argued that the intended referendum is "misconceived, potentially dangerous and should be abandoned". That is because the proposals presented to the government, if approved by referendum, would establish indigenous Australians as a "favoured class". This would be the predictable effect of the proposed section 51A, which includes the sentence: "Acknowledging the need to secure the advancement of Aboriginal and Torres Strait Islander peoples". The phrase "respecting the continuing heritage" could lead to exclusive land claims.

The proposed section 116A, prohibiting racial discrimination by governments, could, Maley suggested, prevent some actions of "national defence, border protection, immigration, the management of civil disorder, international sanctions, or measures such as the recent Northern Territory intervention into Aboriginal settlements."

Maley also pointed to the ethnic bias of the proposed referendum: "Unacknowledged in all of this are those people who created what is 'now known as the Australian nation' and Constitution, and their descendants and their culture that turned a harsh continent into a prosperous homeland for 24 million inhabitants."

The difference in quality between Hosch's and Maley's arguments also characterises the two sides of the debate, between the Recognise campaign and the rising cautionary voices. The difference can be seen by contrasting the Gillard-appointed Expert Panel's *Report* and criticisms of it, including the book edited by Gary Johns, *Recognise What?* The extremity of the Recognise campaign has not moderated in the last month, as illustrated by Noel Pearson's desperate manoeuvres. That campaign is now descending into unreality and absurdity. But the lost contest over s18c raises the prospect that argument will not decide the Constitutional debate either, that reason and freedom, two mutually supporting pillars of democracy, are being undermined by the ethnic divisions produced by diversity.[5]

It is time for those who represent the majority to start playing the multicultural game, by organising their own teams around the principle that free speech and equality before the law are not only Enlightenment but patriotic values, cultural traditions that form part of our national identity. The balance of power might have shifted so far towards the multiculturalism industry that politicians will only rediscover the value of liberal philosophy and prudent constitutionalism when the supporters of those principles can back sentiment with overwhelming votes.

12. 'Recognise' the retreat*

The campaign to recognise Indigenous peoples in the Australian Constitution has descended into chaos. The Prime Minister's hand-picked advisory panel has recommended that yet another advisory body be formed, declaring the public is not yet ready for a referendum. Translated, this means Australians are not guaranteed to vote 'yes' to anything placed before them. The panel has suggested that the referendum be delayed to 2017,[1] the fiftieth anniversary of the successful 1967 referendum. This amounts to dumping the matter in the "too hard" basket.

The government is sending strong signals that a referendum cannot be won in the short term. The Prime Minister indicated last week that a delay would improve the chances of success.[2]

My guess is that the Recognise What? campaign has played a role in confounding the referendum process, by pointing out the irresponsibility of the more ambitious proposals. The book of the same name, edited by Gary Johns, and a growing log of cautionary articles in the media appear to be having the desired

---

*   Originally published: *Quadrant Online*, 15 Sept. 2014.

effect. The panel chairman, former Deputy Prime Minister John Anderson, said he feared the referendum would fail due to extreme demands from Recognise supporters or a scare campaign by conservatives. This remark hints at the depth of the Recognise campaign's confusion. "Scare campaign" is a strange way to characterise opposition to extremism.

Another sign of confusion in the Recognise ranks is Noel Pearson's discarding the recommendations of the Gillard-appointed Expert Panel. This was a costly, time-consuming exercise whose report Pearson approved. It is not something he would lightly abandon. But on September 10 that is what he did[3] — or perhaps pretended to do because his Plan B is almost as risky as the Expert Panel's. Pearson adopted something close to **Greg Craven's proposal** for instituting a new statutory body to give Aborigines quasi-legal oversight on legislation affecting indigenous peoples. And he still demands removal of references to race, despite this being irrelevant to recognition and posing technical nightmares for the drafters of the referendum. This Plan B is being sold by Pearson and the media as a concession to conservatives. But it is radical.

The new proposal reveals a fundamental misunderstanding of the scholarship on ethnicity and nationalism and its application to Australia. Pearson maintains that the Australian nation has three parts: an ancient heritage provided by Indigenous peoples, the political and social structures provided by British settlers, and the joys of cultural diversity provided by post-WWII immigrants. This pretends that Aborigines' heritage, inherited by 2.5% of the population, is claimed by all Australians and that non-Indigenous peoples do not have their own ancient heritages; as if their deep histories were forgotten on arrival on these shores. The British founders provided a core identity as well as structures.

Pearson is not alone in constructing such fantastic historical scenarios. Other commentators claim that white settlement itself was a sin, a "bitter historical injustice", for which the Australian people must permanently atone. This is an outrageous position that denies the legitimacy of the nation's possession of the continent.[4] Pearson's new proposal would establish an ethnic constitution that makes most Australians second-class citizens. Such a fantasy offers no justification[5] for giving Aborigines constitutional privileges, which as Wesley Aird, a member of Recognise What? points out, is the last thing they need.[6]

We should hope that the Recognise campaign's intellectual, political and moral chaos never finds its way into our Constitution.

13. Prisoner Abbott: Referendum Developments[*]

The effort to recognise indigenous peoples in the Constitution is gaining momentum, despite reckless proposals coming from sources such as Opposition Leader Bill Shorten and the racially biased Expert Panel appointed by Julia Gillard. Both want recognition placed in the body of the Constitution. Warren Mundine,[1] head of the Prime Minister's Indigenous Advisory Council, seeks to exploit the referendum to override Mabo (too conservative!) by having governments sign treaties with indigenous peoples.

Pro-recognition arguments are weak. Exponents avoid answering the objections that have been raised. The arguments are getting weaker. Prime Minister Tony Abbott recently called on monarchists to place their trust in him with regard to a referendum, asking his fellow constitutional conservatives to "suspend scepticism" because "I would never seek change unless I was convinced that it would be change for the better." The prime minister's claim to be a conservative is wearing thin. He presents himself as an Anglophile who recognises and

---

[*] Written 11 Dec. 2014.

respects the British origins of the nation, yet recently asserted without qualification that Islam is as much a part of national identity as Protestantism, Catholicism or Judaism.[2] This is the same Prime Minister who allowed an openly ethnic lobby to derail repeal of the anti-free speech section 18C of the Racial Discrimination Act, overturning an election promise and a core conservative principle with the express goal of appeasing the Islamic community. Abbott is a convert[3] to multiculturalism and transformatory levels of immigration whose response to Islamic terrorism was to expand the surveillance state to protect national security but has never canvassed the more fundamental remedy of restricting immigration from affected parts of the world. Abbott does not condemn or question the outrageous "acknowledgment of country" ritual being inflicted on school pupils throughout Australia that offers no recognition of our European pioneers and even withholds affirmation of national sovereignty. This champion of conservative values continued the Gillard government's policy of funding an advertising campaign for one side of the planned recognition referendum, well before the wording of the referendum had been decided. He has even taken to accusing of sexism colleagues critical of his chief of staff, Peta Credlin. After all that, he adds "trust me" to the list of poor arguments for constitutional recognition. Voters should not suspend scepticism towards either major party on matters bearing on identity or cohesion or defence of the majority's ethnic interests. It is time to be alert.

Unfortunately a survey by Polity Research[4] finds that 63 per cent of voters say they are ready to vote, and three quarters of those would vote yes to recognition. Taken together, 47 per cent of voters now say they would vote for recognition. That figure could fall when the referendum question is decided, but it is worrying nevertheless. The new poll indicates a change from three months previously when the prime minister's Indigenous Recognition Advisory Panel reported, after nationwide consultation, that the electorate was not ready to support recognition that gave special treatment to any one group.[5]

Momentum is growing despite the weakness of arguments for recognition because both sides of politics, from the cultural Marxist left to our "conservative" prime minister, support constitutional change. Momentum is helped by the mainstream media, from the Fairfax left to the Murdoch "right", keeping in lockstep in support, and because the government is funding a propaganda campaign that amounts to a blank cheque for whatever measures are put in a referendum. Most of Australia's political and cultural elites are united behind recognition. Even Kerry Jones, former head of Australians for Constitutional Monarchy, has joined with arch republicans such as Tom Keneally to support Mr. Abbott's policy.[6] That is why Aboriginal activist Noel Pearson believes that "highly conservative" leaders such as Tony Abbott are the most useful supporters of his referendum plans, because they have the trust of rural and regional Australia, the Anglo heartland, and can therefore induce them to suspend scepticism.[7] Pearson does not mean that Abbott is conservative in the sense that he himself is – an ethnic leader who puts his people's welfare first – only that Abbott has that image among rural whites. The idea is that Abbott can neutralise Anglo conservative opposition to policies that would incite them to fierce opposition if those policies came from individuals known to hold their identity and values in disdain.

Naturally the pro-recognition forces find it congenial to work together. An example is a story presented by the ABC's *7:30 Report* of 17 September 2014 that amounted to pro-recognition advertising. The story reported prime minister Abbott's announcement that the referendum was to be postponed to 2017, intended to give the Recognise campaign time to convince the electorate and fortuitously coinciding with the successful 1967 referendum on indigenous inclusion in the census.

Comments were garnered from pro-recognition voices – Fred Chaney, member of the aforementioned Expert Panel, Tanya Hosch, joint campaign director of the official Recognise campaign, and Noel Pearson, also of the Expert Panel. Not one critical voice was presented despite several reasoned cautions having been published, such as by Gary Johns[8] and Barry Maley.[9] The segment ended with the Recognise logo and website address, shown on full screen. This was partisanship pure and simple, in violation of the ABC's charter.

What can those sceptical of constitutional recognition do to prevent the Constitution being changed into an ethnically biased instrument of social engineering? They can continue to raise their voices with appeals to reason and prudence. This has been happening. In his recent book, *Democracy in Decline – Steps in the Wrong Direction* (Connor Court Publishing), James Allan has warned that a successful referendum will hand power to activist judges who seek to overturn the wishes of the majority (i.e. circumvent democracy) in the name of "human rights" and transnationalism. (See the excellent review by John Roskam.[10])

Just last week David Flint and Jai Martinkovits replied to Tony Abbott's speech to the Constitutional Monarchists by calling on him to remove the Recognise campaign from its elite handlers and arrange for the election of a constitutional convention that listens to citizens' concerns.[11]

It must worry advocates of recognition that individuals of substance are objecting. Referendum campaigns are fragile, as the prime minister understands. He has stated that if constitutional recognition is to have a chance it must be supported by both major political parties and all state governments. Indeed, the proposal will be at risk if "anyone of any substance" campaigns against the proposal.[12]

It helps to know that clusters of policies rise and fall together. A government that is pro-business in setting the corporate tax rate will tend to favour business in other areas such as tariff policy, perhaps because it is influenced by certain lobbies. It is therefore a bad omen that the Prime Minister retreated from reforming section 18C of the Racial Discrimination Act in the face of a multicultural lobby similar to that demanding constitutional recognition.[13] If Tony Abbott had stood his ground against that lobby, we could have greater confidence in his ability to withstand pressure from the same people in favour of constitutional recognition. Or if he had corrected his erroneous statement about Islam and national identity, we would have reason to trust his ability to deal with identity issues in general. Moreover the truthful and just resolutions of these issues would have helped educate the public, instead of increasing confusion.

Unfortunately it seems the prime minister himself needs educating on matters of identity and history. Looking back at the foundation of the nation Abbott believes it had an "Aboriginal heritage, a British foundation and a multicultural character", and it is these historical identities he wants "reflected in our Constitution".[14] This nonsense bears a striking resemblance to the ideas of Noel Pearson at his worst, ideas that combine ill-informed Aboriginal activism with radical multiculturalism, who holds up president Barack Obama as a model leader of ethnic unity.[15] His own version of these ideas is not quite as absurd as his student's; he more accurately refers to the multicultural element as a recent development and does not pretend to position it as a formative element of the nation. This dash of reality does not save Pearson's analysis or that of his imitator. Even if one accepts Pearson's view that the Australian nation was created by its Constitution in 1901 – an elementary confounding of state with nation – his ideas are hopelessly confused, even when parroted by the prime minister. In 1901 the only Australians who had an Aboriginal heritage were themselves Aboriginal, a situation little changed by 1950 and even today. The Australia of 1901 (or 1950 or 2014) cannot be summarised as having only a "multicultural character" because a majority of the population was and is Anglo-Celtic. The country's alleged diverse identity is actually a variation on the Anglo-Celtic historic identity. In 1901 that was also true subjectively: the nation saw itself as a local variant of British identity. The worst error committed by Pearson and swallowed by our prime minister is that the British supplied only institutions – parliamentary democracy, language, et cetera. This allows them to airbrush Anglo Australians out of the picture of modern Australia, when in fact the majority of Australia's population traces family histories back to Britain and Europe. This is a deeply subversive portrayal of Australian society consistent with what columnist Greg Sheridan describes as the cultural genocide of Anglo Australia. It is not what one expected of a "highly conservative" leader.[16]

Mr. Abbott wants us to celebrate a history fabricated by the Aboriginal and multicultural industries. No upstanding citizen should vote for a referendum predicated on erasing the memory of Australia's pioneers and historic nation. No prime minister should give access to someone like Noel Pearson who promulgates that lie or claims to be nauseated by Anzac Day because it is too white.[17] That sort of hostility directed at the nation and that privileged access would be discouraged if Anglo Australians were respected in multicultural politics or had champions in government, real conservatives. Unless constitutional recognition is to consist of a running commentary on the latest demographic changes imposed on an unwilling country, it should deal exclusively with real origins, not a rainbow armband view of history.

An issue linked to the Recognise campaign is the Acknowledgment of Country ritual (AOC) that is routinely practised in school and public meetings. The ritual is an assault on national identity and territorial sovereignty, by ignoring its pioneers and their descendants' sense of nationhood. This agitprop continues unopposed by the major parties. It represents a strategic gain by the radical left and indigenous activists because the ritual is a referendum in microcosm, recognising Aborigines while derecognising nation and commonwealth.

The Recognise referendum campaign and AOC are linked. The former is more likely to succeed while the latter continues unabated. Conversely, the chances of a successful referendum would be slim were a popular campaign against AOC to emerge beforehand.

The most effective campaign against the Acknowledgment of Country would not seek to abandon but to balance it with recognition of the nation's full historical origins, what might be called an Acknowledgment of Nation. This should affirm the Commonwealth's sovereignty over the continent, recognise the Anglo pioneers and founders of the nation, and recognise the original inhabitants.

Tony Abbott shows signs of having been captured by elements of the Aboriginal and multicultural industries. Those who want the real Tony Abbott back should demand that he earn their trust by repudiating malicious influences and re-affirming his conservatism. That will require not an isolated grand gesture but methodical repositioning. Certain lobbies should be visibly pushed away. Some advisers fired. And some coherent analysis, personal explanation and apology should be presented by Tony Abbott that is grounded in conservative principles.

14. Why the business council of Australia?[*]

Momentum continues to build for constitutional privileging of indigenous Australians in the Constitution. The latest recruit is the Business Council of Australia (BCA), which represents the country's 100 largest companies. In its submission to the Federal Parliament's Joint Select Committee on the planned referendum, the BAC urges the government to clarify the form of words to be put to the electorate and a precise date.[1]

The BAC has assembled its submission from the usual platitudes – such as that privileging Aborigines in the Constitution would advance "reconciliation" without explaining how doing so would reconcile non-indigenous Australians to their subordinate status.

The arguments advanced do not improve on the BCA's previous support for the referendum. For example, in February 2013 the BAC agreed with Parliament's Act of Recognition, arguing that constitutional recognition "could play a valuable role" in closing the "opportunity gap" between indigenous and non-indigenous

---

[*]   Originally published: www.recognisewhat.org.au, 2 Feb. 2015.

Australians. This says nothing and contributes nothing, like the radical Gillard-appointed Expert Panel.

A business angle is indicated by the following: "Recognising and valuing Indigenous heritage and culture is part of building the kind of relationships that allow us to work together more effectively, and to solve problems and improve outcomes for everyone." As James Allan argues in his new book, *Democracy in Decline*, the more likely outcome is that litigation will grow and activist judges be given rein, reducing the power of parliaments to govern.

Where the BCA attempts to invoke principle, it merely exposes the hypocrisy of the Recognise campaign. "True reconciliation involves acknowledging our nation's history and the special place of Aboriginal and Torres Strait Islander peoples as the first Australians, alongside practical actions to improve people's living standards." Recognise the nation's history? That is the last thing on the mind of the Recognise push and, it seems, the BCA's leadership. Such recognition would describe the First Fleet and the pioneers who made the country through risk and toil, and who invented the Commonwealth to protect the nation they had created. A genuine recognition of the nation's history would include Aborigines but not pretend that they are the whole story.

It is a mystery why so august and realistic a body as the Business Council of Australia would align itself with such shoddy analysis and shameful goals. Its members should demand that the BCA oppose any referendum that insults and disadvantages the nation.

15. Genes and Aboriginality*

To the Editor
16 February 2015

Regarding the article, "Brawl over 'wannabe' and 'tick-the-box' Aborigines", Feb. 16.

The mainstream politically correct definition of Aboriginality – based on subjective belief and social belonging – is meant to be more inclusive than strict criteria of descent and race. Andrew Bolt was met with outrage and punitive judicial activism when he asserted that descent and race are valid criteria for deciding Aboriginality.

Yet Clyde Mansell, Chairman of the Aboriginal Land Council of Tasmania, thinks that the accepted definition poses a threat to his people because individuals who don't care about the Aboriginal community could take control. In recent years 19 new Aboriginal organisations have been registered in Tasmania as eligible to receive federal grants, in line with a rapid rise in

---

*   An unpublished letter-to-the-editor, 16 Feb. 2015.

the number of people claiming to be Aboriginals. Mansell wants true Aboriginals to "combat" pseudo Aboriginals by making it more difficult for the latter to be recognised by governments. "The real question of who's in and who's out is going to be the most important issue facing our community", Mansell stated. He suggests adding the criterion of continual involvement with the community.

Rodney Dillon, a prominent Tasmanian Aboriginal, disagrees. He believes that DNA testing is preferable because it would keep false claimants out while admitting those who have recently discovered their Aboriginal descent. Members of the Stolen Generation would be admitted by genetic tests but not by Mansell's criteria, he claims. "DNA testing is pure. It's foolproof. It would prove once and for all who is Aboriginal."

Mansell and Dillon are at cross purposes. Mansell is concerned with commitment to the community and wants rigorous standards of identity to serve that end. Dillon is concerned with inclusion and therefore wants to adopt an easily-met criterion of identity.

This is a difficult matter to decide because ethnicity depends on all of these criteria – descent, shared culture and commitment. And they are interrelated. For example, genetic testing measures shared descent, a universal of ethnic identity. And commitment is usually strongest among those with family connections to the community. Rodney Dillon alluded to this when he urged acceptance of genetically certified Aboriginals as "our brothers and sisters", members of the one "family". Conversely, ignoring relatedness by descent as an identity criterion will inevitably dilute kinship and thus commitment.

Dillon's proposal to use DNA testing is valid as a necessary though not a sufficient condition for claiming Aboriginality.

16. Recognise campaign in disarray[*]

Why has Noel Pearson broken ranks with the Expert Panel's recommendations for a constitutional amendment? Was not the Panel composed of experts? At considerable cost to the taxpayer, this august body was touted as a reservoir of mature indigenous activists and white sympathisers of stature and wisdom.

Now Pearson concedes one of the most elementary criticisms of the Recognise agenda, admitting that the constitution is not the appropriate place for symbolism and poetry. This opinion leader, who is given Page One praise by the mainstream media, now realises that the Constitution is a rule book. A few short years ago he was insisting that constitutional recognition would cure Aborigines of their multiple health problems; that lack of recognition was the "ultimate explanation" of their disability.[1] He even thought that recognition would improve educational outcomes and make Aborigines more innovative and entrepreneurial. Perhaps it was easy for Pearson to dispense with these claims because they had no empirical foundation (see Chapter 3). Pearson and the Expert Panel were reflecting the corruption of the social sciences, evidenced by leftist

---

[*]   Originally published: www.RecogniseWhat.org.au, 16 April 2015.

academics driving biology out of the curriculum.[2] Pearson's and the Panel's problem was not that they were disengaged from the academic establishment. If anything they were too reliant on it. The Royal Australian and New Zealand College of Psychiatry, the Western Australian Centre for Health Promotion Research, and the Lowitja Institute all claimed, absurdly, that constitutional recognition was critical to close the gap, especially in health. They and the Business Council of Australia, which with Quantas and other corporate sponsors has also uncritically supported the Recognise campaign's inflated claims, should take a hard businesslike look at themselves.

The Panel's credibility is on the line. Co-chair Mark Leibler and Panel member Fred Chaney appear genuinely shocked at Pearson's desertion. If the Panel's report is not a sinking ship, if Leibler and Chaney still believe in their own analysis and recommendations, they should promptly reaffirm them and summarise the supporting evidence. That would be difficult because the Panel was a political exercise, not a scholarly one.

Pearson's credibility is also in doubt, a situation not rescued by his plan B. Instead of constitutional recognition, he now states, there should be a declaration of recognition by the Parliament combined with the establishment of a new Aboriginal body that Parliament is required to consult before passing legislation affecting Aboriginal or Torres Strait Islanders.[3] The race clauses "should be replaced with an indigenous power" such that ". . . Parliament . . . be required procedurally to consult with and consider the advice of an indigenous body in its lawmaking for indigenous affairs". Senate seats might be reserved for indigenous representatives. As conservative commentator Geoffrey Partington states in a letter to *The Australian* (16 April 2015), Pearson's complaints about exclusion and discrimination against Aborigines in the Constitution are without foundation.[4] And as James Paterson argues in the same newspaper, Pearson's recommendation is even more radical than constitutional recognition because it would more grievously divide the nation by race and compromise the legitimacy of government.[5] One might add that it would also empower and enrich the Aboriginal and Multicultural industries to the nation's detriment.

These criticisms omit to take into consideration the political environment in which the Recognise campaign was conceived. Since the 1970s Australia has been in the grip of a wider and more powerful influence, multiculturalism, that has helped radicalise immigration policy, thus feeding minority ethnic activism including the Aboriginal industry. Multiculturalism cannot be overlooked as an asset of socialist and "green" agendas. It is transforming the country in the direction of ever greater diversity, a proven toxin for civil liberties and social cohesion. The multicultural lobby supports the recognition campaign and the restriction of civil liberties, for example by defeating the Government's mandate to reform section 18C of the Racial Discrimination Act.[6] The multicultural-immigration axis is committing what conservative columnist Greg Sheridan calls the "cultural genocide" of Anglo Australia.[7] Establishment support for constitutional recognition should be viewed in that broader context of elite ethnic politics.

From that perspective, Pearson's new proposals commit the same error as the Expert Panel by discriminating against Australia's true national history. If historical recognition of some kind is warranted for the country's first peoples, the same is deserved by the first nation, our core Anglo identity, which provided Australia's demographic, cultural, and economic foundations and continued to do so until as recently as the 1970s and beyond. If Aborigines need special representation to prevent their marginalisation, the same applies to the one ethnic group excluded from multicultural forums, vilified in school curricula and steadily displaced by immigration imposed without democratic consent.

Hopefully the movement to hold a referendum on recognition will collapse. But if the Recognise campaign manages to force a referendum, national identity and Australia's unjust ethnic hierarchy should be placed firmly on the table.

17. The Pearson Factor[*]

Noel Pearson's recently stated opinions about the goals of constitutional recognition should concern constitutional conservatives and, indeed, anyone who values truth. He was speaking on the ABC's *Lateline* on July 6, 2015. The following exchange occurred towards the end of his **interview** with Emma Alberici.[1]

ALBERICI: *Do you really think [your children are] held back in any way whatsoever just because of a few words in the Constitution?*

PEARSON: *Um, yeah – well at the moment, for example, we're characterised as a race. That's what the Constitution characterises us, and it infects our whole psychology, not just the blackfellas, the whitefellas too, 'cause the whitefellas think we're a separate race and treat us as a race, an illegitimate idea, and we ourselves have internalised that.*

We think of ourselves as a separate race. I think the moment we move to recognition of Indigenous first nations we'll enter

---

[*] Originally published: *Quadrant Online* 22 July 2015.

a phase where race will just be a concept from the 19th and 20th century that we put behind us, and we as black fellas won't have this negative idea of race about ourselves and hopefully the wider community will stop having low expectations of us.

These are not off-the-cuff ideas of Pearson's. He has expressed the same for years, from before the release of the Expert Panel's 2012 *Report* on constitutional recognition, of which he was a contributing author. His insistence on abstruse ideological notions of race feel like non sequiturs spliced in from a different debate.[2] They are not only flawed but irrelevant to indigenous interests, as documented in my three-part *Quadrant* essay on the Report reproduced in chapters 3-5 of the present volume.[3]

The flaws are:

Firstly, the Constitution's reference to "race" was formulated before "ethnicity" came into use in the social sciences. "Race" is now limited in meaning to genetically caused characteristics, usually of continental-scale populations. But in 1900 the term covered other meanings as well, including ethnic populations. So, taken historically, the Constitution refers to Indigenous Australians as ethnic groups, which they are.

Secondly, nothing in the Constitution "infects our whole psychology". It is a marginal influence on Australian culture. It is ridiculous to suggest that the Constitution makes people think that Indigenous peoples are ethnic groups (or races). Social psychological research indicates that by age three normally developing children distinguish races as descent groups.[4] Not many children are familiar with the Australian Constitution. Humans are well equipped to distinguish races and ethnicities. They don't need to be told by anthropologists or sociologists or constitutions that these categories exist.

Thirdly, race is not an "illegitimate" concept but an observational one. It can be an inadmissible distinction in some settings, for example in public administration. It is only illegitimate as a concept in the rarefied domain of cultural Marxist ideology, which unfortunately often includes the curriculum taught to university students in the humanities and soft social sciences. Race and ethnicity are everyday facts about humans. A person's ethnic ancestry can be identified by genes alone, and genetic kinship within ethnic groups is typically equivalent to that of first cousins.[5] Aborigines and other Australian voters might be surprised to learn that a leader of the Recognise campaign does not believe that his ethnic family, or any ethnic family, has a racial component.

Indigenous Australians are losing their racial distinctiveness as they marry other races. Ethnic identity can continue well beyond the blurring of racial differences because it is largely based on beliefs about descent. Ethnicity is also constituted by distinctive culture, which many Aborigines and Torres Strait Islanders are also losing as they assimilate to the mainstream. That process might be regretted by ethnic loyalists, such as Pearson, but it does not make race or ethnicity illegitimate ideas.

Fourthly, combining the preceding points, it is not the Constitution that makes Aborigines think of themselves as a separate ethnicity. They have that belief because they do not think the way Noel Pearson says they should, and neither does he. When he refers to "blackfellas" and "whitefellas" he speaks more sense than is found in his radical anthropology. Recognising Indigenous peoples in the Constitution will not prevent fellas, white or black, from thinking in terms of race and ethnicity. And it will do nothing to alter expectations while Indigenous Australians continue to experience medical, social and economic disabilities that are not at all caused by the Constitution but by historical, cultural and genetic factors.

From where did someone as astute as Pearson acquire such confused notions? The Expert Panel's co-chair, Mark Leibler, who mentored the young Pearson's law career, expresses similar views. Also, the politicisation of legal studies curricula has been proceeding for generations. Law professors can be as ignorant of elementary ethnography and biology as other humanities graduates. As recently as 2010 a senior Australian academic lawyer claimed that Australia's border protection was racist because, he thought, borders were not important in traditional societies.[6] Ideas similar to those of Pearson and Leibler are expressed in the Expert Panel Report, which based them in part on the anthropologist Ashley Montagu, an apologist for Stalin and vilifier of Western culture.[7] It would be unfortunate if communist propaganda on racial and ethnic affairs found its way into the Australian Constitution.

Noel Pearson is a leading Indigenous proponent of constitutional recognition for Indigenous Australians. Despite (or perhaps because of) his open ethnic activism, it seems his every utterance is featured by the mainstream media and not only for political reasons. He is articulate, learned in Indigenous affairs, possessed of a legally trained mind, charismatic.

This prominence means that the success of the Recognise project rests disproportionately on Pearson's shoulders. Should he present a powerful case to voters, they are more likely to vote for recognition. But if he commits a major blunder the overall project could suffer. Symbols and symbolic leaders mean a lot in politics.

Over the last few years Pearson has advanced a number of radical proposals, without attracting much criticism from media commentators or politicians. For example, recently he upped the Recognise ante by demanding more than recognition in the Constitution. In his view a body elected by Indigenous people –

an ethnic parliament – should be empowered to review all legislation affecting them and make recommendations to the government. This proposal is meant to appeal to conservatives, yet it is one of the most radical ideas put forward. An Aboriginal parliament would necessarily be supported by a dedicated bureaucracy and have a voice in public affairs much greater than the existing Indigenous claims industry. It would further separate Aboriginal peoples from the rest of society and advance the apparent goal of reversing the British annexation of the continent upon which the Australian nation is based.

Professor **Marcia Langton** recently warned that, should a No campaign receive funding, the Recognise referendum will be defeated.[8] Pearson's irrationality and radicalism on the subject of race and Indigenous privilege are likely to be main targets of that campaign. Recognise's most visible advocate could become the No campaign's greatest asset.

18. Now It's Indigenous-Only Constitutional Conventions[*]

Once again Tony Abbott's sound instincts have been overwhelmed by Australia's inverted ethnic hierarchy.

The federal government has caved into Noel Pearson's demand for indigenous Australians to have their own series of constitutional conventions, funded by tax payers. The remainder of the population will be offered mixed "mainstream" meetings.[1] The two sets of consultative meetings will be conducted in parallel. Mr Abbott's first impulse was to keep the meetings inclusive, to avoid a "them and us" procedure. He has retreated from this wise caution, though he did maintain a stand against holding the indigenous conventions before the mainstream meetings.

The agreement to fund indigenous-only forums is a dangerous precedent. Consider how it might lead to other demands.

It could be argued that, while all citizens should participate in discussing the Recognise proposals, Anglo Australians have a special duty to do so because they connect us to our colonial

---

[*]   Originally published: www.RecogniseWhat.org.au, 24 Aug. 2015.

past and remain at the heart of our national identity. At the same time they are the majority of the population, the leading culture in numbers and links to the nation's past. The argument could continue by asserting that as the leading culture Anglo Australians have a special responsibility to correct past wrongs and protect the national interest. Such a special role was implicitly recognised in the Expert Panel appointed by the Gillard Government, which consisted largely of indigenous and Anglo Australians.

Fairness and symbolism (though not common sense) would seem to dictate that if indigenous Australians have their own forums, Anglo Australians should have theirs, because it is *their* burden of guilt for alleged past wrongs that the Recognise campaign is designed to correct. Australia was a consciously British-derived society until after well after the Second World War.

If the prospect of Anglo-only conventions seems outrageously discriminatory, why did our Prime Minister agree to indigenous-only ones? Will the media highlight instances of non-indigenous Australians being barred from meetings or prevented from speaking? Will bureaucrats establish a working group to accredit attendees by race? Perhaps badges will be issued showing a large "I" for indigenous people, and an "O" for other ethnicities. No, that would be too easy to fake. Can we look forward to federal police at the door checking racial ID? DNA tests can now be done quickly.

The government's decision to racially segregate discussion of the Recognise campaign – that is the reality – should shock Australians. But it is part of a wider trend of privileging indigenous activists. Indigenous Australians now have their own free-to-air television channel, a privilege denied other ethnic groups. Every day, school students across the nation are subjected to indoctrination that symbolically dispossesses their people. In a country with dozens of ethnic groups – multicultural Australia – students sit through "acknowledgement of country" rituals in which the land is designated as belonging to a tiny minority. There is no mention of the nation's pioneers and settlers, of those who explored, named, and forged modern Australia. School assemblies do not affirm most students' place in Australia.

The government's decision to further racialise an already discriminatory recognition process is akin to its back-down on reform of section 18c of the Racial Discrimination Act. That surrender was made in the face of fierce lobbying from the multicultural community and its "progressive" allies.[2] The government has sound instincts but was let down by intellectual weakness in the field of ethnic affairs, which can be traced to the politicisation of the humanities and social sciences since the 1960s.[3]

It's time the government began to think about the Recognise campaign outside the box. A good start would be for Tony Abbott to trust his instincts.

19. Gillard's Ghost: The new Referendum Council*

The new Referendum Council planned by the Abbott government has been appointed by the Turnbull government, in cooperation with the Labor Opposition led by Bill Shorten.[1] The Council is an eminent group charged with guiding the national discussion on constitutional recognition of indigenous Australians, and advising political leaders on progress and next steps.

The Council appears to suffer from the same ethnic imbalance as its predecessor, the Expert Panel appointed by Labor prime minister Julia Gillard. The new group has the same leaders as the old, Aboriginal leader Patrick Dodson and Jewish community leader Mark Leibler. The other 14 members consist of 7 indigenous and 7 non-indigenous Australians, a 50-50 ratio. The following biographical details are taken from the official announcement.[2]

---

* Originally published: www.RecogniseWhat.com.au, 8 Dec. 2015.

INDIGENOUS	NON-INDIGENOUS
Patrick Dodson, Chair of the Yawuru Native Title Company	Mark Leibler AC, tax lawyer, Chairman, Australia/Israel and Jewish Affairs Council
Pat Anderson AO, outgoing CEO of the Lowitja Foundation	Andrew Demetriou, former CEO of the Australian Football League
Megan Davis, Director, Indigenous Law Centre, University of NSW	Natasha Stott Despoja AM, Australian Ambassador for Women and Girls, former Democrats Party Senator for South Australia.
Mick Gooda, Aboriginal and Torres Strait Islander Justice Commissioner	Murray Gleeson AC QC – former Chief Justice of the High Court of Australia
Tanya Hosch, Joint Campaign Director of Recognise.	Linda Keneally, former Labor Party Premier of New South Wales.
Noel Pearson, lawyer, co-founder of the Cape York Land Council.	Jane McAloon, business adviser, former President of Governance and Group Company Secretary of BHP Billiton.
Dalassa Yorkston, CEO of the Torres Shire Council.	Michael Rose, CEO of Allens law firm and Chairman of the Business Council of Australia's Indigenous Engagement Taskforce.
Galarrwuy Yunupingu AM, Elder of the Gumatj clan of the Yolngu people. Former Chairman of the Northern Land Council.	Amanda Vanstone, former Liberal Senator for South Australia, former Liberal Party Minister for Immigration and Multicultural Affairs.

Continuity between the original Panel and the new Council is aided by five common members: Davis, Dodson, Gooda, Leibler, and Pearson.

Ideological continuity is also assisted by Professor Davis, who is Chair of the United Nation's Permanent Forum on Indigenous Issues.[3] She helps tie the referendum process to the 2007 United Nations Declaration on the Rights of Indigenous Peoples, as was the report of the Expert Panel. The Declaration was declined by the Howard government but ratified by the Gillard government. It is a deeply irrational and divisive document whose recommendations for indigenous autonomy and ethnic discrimination contradict the UN's equally contentious Convention on the Elimination of All Forms of Racial Discrimination. (I analysed these documents as part of a review of the Gillard Expert Panel, reproduced in Chapter 4 of the present volume.)[4] The incompetence and extremism of the Expert Panel's report was partly due to its reliance on the UN's cultural Marxism as well as on the writings of Ashley Montagu, the pro-Soviet anthropologist given to vilifying the West. It is not at all reassuring that five individuals who signed off on such a document were reappointed to the new Advisory Council.

What was the Turnbull government thinking? Why the convergence with one of Julia Gillard's most ill-considered policies? It is unwise for Australia to allow its civil liberties and domestic peace to be compromised by globalist agendas. And it is imprudent for Malcolm Turnbull, who is vulnerable to the accusation of corporate arrogance, to be seen embracing such agendas.

Continuity between the Panel and Council is also evidenced by retention of the same ethnic bias. The Recognise campaign is thoroughly racialised. Yet no representation is given to Australia's burgeoning Asian and Islamic communities. On the indigenous side, it might seem appropriate that all of the

Council's indigenous members are community leaders, with long track records of ethnic activism in the service of their peoples. But why exclude indigenous Australians opposed to the Recognise campaign? And why must most if not all of the non-indigenous members be favourably disposed towards indigenous recognition? Some have gone further by advocating indigenous causes. Only Murray Gleeson appears to have the combination of independence and legal training to act as a brake on the ideological and ethnic enthusiasms of the other members.

Not one member has any history of opposing constitutional recognition, let alone advocating for Anglo or white interests. This asymmetry is completely normal for multiculturalism, which is based on domination of the majority and avoidance of democratic choice. But it is remarkable that the majority goes unrepresented in a referendum process focused on ethnic identity. After all, the point of the referendum is to import ethnicity into a Constitution that does not even name the country's founding Anglo nation. The referendum is being sold as a corrective to past Anglo misdeeds which need to be righted. The recognition campaign is run by people whose ethnic identities are much stronger than the average Australian's. Even the Abbott government approved segregating the consultation process, with indigenous-only meetings.

This hyper-tribal process excludes representatives of Australia's most important tribe, the historic Australian nation.

The practical political question is whether this farce can be pulled off with a straight face. Ordinary Australians are liable to crack up, and not with mirth. My guess is that the referendum will be at risk if the Recognise campaign fails to block funding for the NO campaign.

Endnotes

1. Introduction

1   Quoted in full-page advertisement, *The Australian*, 1 Dec. 2017, p. 9. "We seek constitutional reforms . . ."

2   Windschuttle, K. (2017). *The break-up of Australia: The real agenda behind Aboriginal recognition.* Sydney: Quadrant Books.

3   Salter, F. K. (2008). Evolutionary analyses of ethnic solidarity: An overview. *People and Place, 16*(2), 15-25.

3. Misguided – Part 1

1   Salter, F. K. and H. Harpending (2012). "J. P. Rushton's theory of ethnic nepotism." *Personality and Individual Differences* http://www.sciencedirect.com/science/article/pii/S0191886912005569.
Salter, F. K. (2007/2003). *On genetic interests. Family, ethnicity, and humanity in an age of mass migration.* New York, Transaction, p. 68.

2   *Recognising Aboriginal and Torres Strait Islander Peoples in the Constitution. Report of the Expert Panel.* January 2012. http://www.recognise.org.au/uploads/assets/3446%20FaHCSIA%20ICR%20report_text_Bookmarked%20PDF%2012%20Jan%20v4.pdf

3   A point summary of the Expert Panel's recommendations is provided at: http://www.recognise.org.au/expert-panel-report, accessed 25 June 2013. The full set of recommended amendments is listed in the *Report* on p. xviii.

4   *Report*, p. 153.

5   "$1.3bn deal ends native title dispute", *Weekend Australian*, 6-7 July 2013, p. 2. "Noongar leaders . . . said they were determined that some earnings from the perpetual trust should be used to help reconnect young people with their culture and language because the loss of those things had caused huge problems."

6   "Julia Gillard switch on first peoples referendum", *The Australian*, 20 Sept. 2012. http://www.theaustralian.com.au/national-affairs/policy/julia-gillard-switch-on-first-peoples/story-fn9hm1pm-1226477677329, accessed 25 Oct. 2013.

7   *Report*, p. xviii.

8   *Report*, p. xii.

9   *Report*, p. 14. Section 25 reads: "For the purposes of the last section, if by the law of any State all persons of any race are disqualified from voting at elections for the more numerous House of the Parliament of the State, then, in reckoning the number of the people of the State or of the Commonwealth, persons of that race resident in that State shall not be counted."

10   "Historic Constitution vote over indigenous recognition facing hurdles", *The Australian*, 20 Jan. 2012. http://www.theaustralian.com.au/national-affairs/policy/historic-constitution-vote-over-indigenous-recognition-facing-hurdles/story-fn9hm1pm-1226248879375, accessed 25 Oct. 2013. "Julia Gillard switch on first peoples referendum", *op cit.*

11   Phillip Adams, "Echoes of apartheid", *The Weekend Australian Magazine*, 10 Aug. 2013, p. 38. "Our refugee policies are an echo of the White Australia Policy. They are aimed at brown people. They are aimed at Muslims."

12   "Minister cuts African refugee intake", *The Age*, 2 Oct. 2007. http://www.theage.com.au/articles/2007/10/01/1191091031242.html, accessed 26 Oct. 2013.

13   Salter, F. K. (2010). "The misguided advocates of open borders." *Quadrant* 54(6). http://www.quadrant.org.au/magazine/issue/2010/6/the-misguided-advocates-of-open-borders. Salter, F. K. (2008). "Evolutionary analyses of ethnic solidarity: An overview." *People and Place* 16(2): 15-25.

14   The Australian Literacy and Numeracy Foundation, Fact page, https://wallofhands.com.au/Home/Facts, accessed 20 June 2013.

15   E.g. "'People are just drinking themselves to death'", *The Australian*, 23 April 2013, pp. 1, 6. "Stepping softly no solution: Petrol sniffing is destroying Aboriginal communities", *Weekend Australian*, 28-29 July 2012, Inquirer, p. 17.

16   *Report*, p. xx.

17   Noel Pearson, "Constitutional reform crucial to indigenous wellbeing", *The Weekend Australian*, 24-25 Dec. 2011, p. 20.

18   Ian Smith and Natasha Stott Despoja, "A need to formally recognise First People", *The Australian*, 8 July 2013, p. 10. Subtitle: "There's a strong case for amending the Constitution".

19   *Report*, p. 40.

20 *Report*, pp. 40-41, Lowitja Institute on p. 50. The Western Australian Centre for Health Promotion Research submission is at: http://www.recognise.org.au/uploads/have_your_say/8e3c240f1a b3060a9545.pdf. The Royal Australian and New Zealand College of Psychiatrists' submission is at: http://www.ranzcp.org/Files/ranzcp-attachments/Resources/College_Statements/Position_Statements/ps68-pdf.aspx.

21 Royal Australian and New Zealand College of Psychiatry, quoted in *Report*, p. 40.

22 Amos Aikman, "Indigenous leaders urge change", *The Weekend Australian*, 10-11 Aug. 2013, p. 1.

23 *Report*, p. 50.

24 http://www.lowitja.org.au/, accessed 28 July 2013.

25 Howse, G. (2011). *Legally invisible—How Australian laws impede stewardship and governance for Aboriginal and Torres Strait Islander health*. Melbourne, The Lowitja Institute. http://www.lowitja.org.au/sites/default/files/docs/Legally_Invisible_report.pdf, accessed 29 July 2013.

26 Howse, *Legally invisible*, p. 2.

27 Howse, *Legally invisible*, p. 30.

28 Howse, *Legally invisible*, p. 31.

29 Howse, *Legally invisible*, p. 1.

30 Howse, *Legally invisible*, p. 16.

31 Howse, *Legally invisible*, pp. 18-19.

32 Howse, *Legally invisible*, p. 12.

33 Howse, *Legally invisible*, p. 5.

34 Howse, *Legally invisible*, p. 5.

35 Howse, *Legally invisible*, p. 31.

36 Pat Anderson, "Racism a driver of ill health", *Weekend Australian*, 27-28 July 2013, p. 20.

37 Burke, E. (1790). Reflections on revolution in France. *Essays by Edmund Burke*. E. Burke (ed.). Melbourne, E. W. Cole: , 16-48, p. 37.

38 *Report*, p. 40.

39 Hughes, H. (2007). *Lands of shame*. St Leonards, Centre for Independent Studies. Helen Hughes and Mark Hughes, 2013, "With apologies, PM, home ownership is the key", *The Australian*, 15 Feb., p. 10.

40 The potential for rapid human evolution was originally advanced by E. O. Wilson, who advanced the "thousand year rule" (meaning 1,000 to 10,000 years) for significant change under moderate selection pressure.
Wilson, E. O. (1971). Competitive and aggressive behavior. *Man and beast: Comparative social behavior*. J. F. Eisenberg and W. S. Dillon. Washington DC, Smithsonian Institution Press: 183-217, pp. 204-8.

41 Cochran, G. and H. Harpending (2009). *The 10,000 year explosion: How civilization accelerated human evolution*. New York, Basic Books.

42 Dr. Alan Barclay was interviewed by Alan Jones, Radio 2GB, 9 July 2012.

43 Nicolas Rothwell, "Genes key to health gone awry", *Weekend Australian*, 1-2 June 2013, Inquirer, p. 15.

44 Penman, J. (2013 in preparation). *Biohistory: Epigenetics and the Decline of the West.*

Guccione, L., E. Djouma, J. Penman and A. G. Paolini (2013). "Calorie restriction inhibits relapse behaviour and preference for alcohol within a two-bottle free choice paradigm in the alcohol preferring (iP) rat." *Physiology & Behavior* 110-111: 34-41. http://www.sciencedirect.com/science/article/pii/S003193841200 4064

45 Clark, G. (2007). *A farewell to alms: A brief economic history of the world*. Princeton, NJ, Princeton University Press.

46 Lynn, R. (2005). *Race differences in intelligence: An evolutionary analysis*. Augusta, GA, Washington Summit Publishers, pp. 110-11. Lynn's meta-analysis yields an average of 78 for mixed-race Aborigines, plus a 2 point deficit due to malnutrition.

47 Trzaskowski, M., J. Yang, P. M. Visscher and R. Plomin (2013). "DNA evidence for strong genetic stability and increasing heritability of intelligence from age 7 to 12." *Molecular Psychiatry* (online), 29 Jan., 5 pp.

48 Pearson, "Constitutional reform crucial".

49 For example, a $1.5 billion employment scheme attempted in remote communities failed to prevent absenteeism and drunkenness. "Aboriginal jobs program a complete disaster: Scullion", *The Australian*, 18 Oct. 2013, p. 6.

50 Calculated using the website http://www.mathportal.org/calculators/statistics-calculator/normal-distribution-calculator.php, accessed 10 July 2013. Assumptions: White mean = 98; standard deviation = 15 (as for Aborigines).

51   Gottfredson identifies the threshold IQs for various occupations and activities. Students with IQ 112 or above are best able to manage university courses.
Gottfredson, L. S. (2006). Social consequences of group differences in cognitive ability [http://www.udel.edu/educ/gottfredson/reprints/2004socialconse quences.pdf]. *Introducau a psicologia das diferencas individuais.* C. E. Flores-Mendoza and R. Colom (Eds.). Porto Allegre, Brazil, ArtMed: 433-45. MS available at; http://www.udel.edu/educ/gottfredson/reprints/2004socialconseq uences.pdf, accessed 14 July 2013, p. 41.

52   Catherine Isaac, "Education's fresh charter", *The Australian*, 23 July 2013, p. 12.

53   Lynn's review of tests of Maori IQ yields an average of 90. *Race differences in intelligence*, p. 117.

54   The *Report* discussed the advantages of indigenous treaties in Canada, New Zealand and elsewhere but for tactical reasons recommended against this for Australia at the present time. It would likely "confuse many Australians, and . . . jeopardise public support for [our] other recommendations" (p. 201).

55   Lynn, R. and T. Vanhanen (2002). *IQ and the wealth of nations.* Westport, Conn., Praeger.

56   Benyamin, B. et al. (2013). "Childhood intelligence is heritable, highly polygenic and associated with FNBP1L." *Molecular psychiatry.* http://www.nature.com/mp/journal/vaop/ncurrent/full/mp20121 84a.html.

57   Figueredo, A. J., T. C. d. Baca and M. A. Woodley (2013). "The measurement of human life history strategy." *Personality and Individual Differences* 55: 251–255.

58   Jensen, A. (1998). *The g factor.* Westport, Conn., Praeger. Chapter "The g nexus", pp. 544-583.

59   Spearman, C. (1904). "General intelligence, objectively determined and measured." *The American Journal of Psychology* 15(2): 201-292. http://www.psych.umn.edu/faculty/waller/classes/FA2010/Readin gs/Spearman1904.pdf.

60   Jensen, *The g factor*, pp. 572-8.

61   Woodley, M. and A. J. Figueredo (2013). *Historic variability in heritable general intelligence: Its evolutionary origins and socio-cultural consequences*, The University of Buckingham Press.

62   Lynn, *Race differences in intelligence.* Trzaskowski et al., "DNA evidence".

63 Helen Hughes in *Lands of Shame* quoted by Nicolas Rothwell, "Visionary economist shed light on the plight of Aborigines" *The Australian*, 17 June 2013, p. 3.

64 Ibid.

65 Tony Abbott has stated that stepped-up government support for Aborigines should continue "at least until they have . . . more-or-less comparable educational, employment, housing and health outcomes as the community at large". "Abbott reconciliation pledge", *The Australian* 15 March 2013, pp. 1, 2. Abbott has also announced more achievable goals aimed at providing opportunities: "[A]ll children go to school, all the adults are working or in work-like programs and the ordinary rule of law runs through those communities". Reported by Dennis Shanahan, "Abbott: my pledge to close gap", *The Weekend Australian*, 10-11 Aug. 2013, p. 1.

66 *Report*, p. 42.

67 Mark Leibler, "Racism still shadows our history", *The Sydney Morning Herald*, 20 Jan. 2012. http://www.fpp.co.uk/online/98/07/articles/Leibler100798.html, accessed 5 Aug. 2013.

68 *Official record of the proceedings and debates of the Australasian Federation Conference, 1890*. Melbourne, Robert S. Brain, Government Printer, p. 71.

69 *Official record*, p. 164.

70 Peter Coleman, "Australian notes", *The Spectator Australia*, 5 May 2012, p. vi.

71 Connor, W. (1978). "A nation is a nation, is a state, is an ethnic group, is a . . ." *Ethnic and Racial Studies* 1(4): 378-400.

72 "Dodson calls for new wave of crusaders", *The Australian*, 13 Feb. 2013, pp. 1-2.

73 "Dodson calls for new wave of crusaders", *The Australian*, 13 Feb. 2013, pp. 1-2.

74 Ibid.

75 "Abbott's reconciliation pledge", *The Australian*, 15 March 2013, p. 1.

76 "Abbott reconciliation pledge".

77 "Abbott laments failure on treaty", *The Australian*, 14 Feb. 2013, p. 2.

78 Noel Pearson, 2010, "Hope 2010: Crisis, catharsis, renewal", speech delivered at the Sydney Festival, 13 January.

79 "Reconciliation plea for native title review", *The Australian*, 5 June 2012, p. 9. And see Mick Gooda, "Native title reform could go closer

to fulfilling Mabo's legacy", *The Sydney Morning Herald*, 4 June 2012, p. 9.

80   Walker Connor. (1993). "Beyond reason: The nature of the ethnonational bond." *Ethnic and Racial Studies* 16(3): 373-389.

81   Novak, M. (1996/1971). *Unmeltable ethnics. Politics & culture in American life*. New Brunswick and London, Transaction.

      The remarkable gene maps produced by L. Cavalli-Sforza and colleagues in their 1994 classic, *The history and geography of human genes*, are based on specimens collected on the basis of individuals identifying themselves as pure-blood aborigines of their region (Section 1.9, p. 25).

82   Hobsbawm, E. and T. Ranger, Eds. (1992/1983). *The invention of tradition*. Cambridge, Cambridge University Press.

83   Castles, S., B. Cope, M. Kalantzis and M. Morrissey (1992). *Mistaken identity: Multiculturalism and the demise of nationalism in Australia*. Sydney, Pluto Press, p. 367.

84   Eibl-Eibesfeldt, I. (1989/1984). *Human ethology*. New York, Aldine de Gruyter, pp. 321-34.

85   Keith, A. (1968/1947). *A new theory of human evolution*. New York, Philosophical Library, pp. 316-17.

86   Smith, A. D. (1986). *The ethnic origins of nations*. Oxford, Basil Blackwell.

      Kaufmann, E. P. (2004). Dominant ethnicity: From background to foreground. *Rethinking ethnicity: Majority groups and dominant minorities*. E. P. Kaufmann. London, Routledge: 1-14.

87   Gat, A. and A. Yakobson (2013). *Nations. The long history and deep roots of political ethnicity and nationalism*. Cambridge, Cambridge University Press, pp. 278-9.

88   Toft, M. D. (2003). *The geography of ethnic violence: Identity, interests, and the indivisibility of territory*. Princeton, Princeton University Press. "[E]thnic groups want to control territory because it means securing their identity. A secure identity, in turn, means the group's continued existence and survival." (p. 31).

      Sirin, C. V. (2011). "Is it cohesion or diversion? Domestic instability and the use of force in international crises." *International Political Science Review* 32(3): 303-321.

89   Salter, F. K., Ed. (2004). *Welfare, ethnicity, & altruism: New data & evolutionary theory*. London, Frank Cass.

90   http://www.psychology.org.au/Assets/Files/Welcome-to-and-Acknolwedgement-of-Country.pdf, accessed 18 July 2013.

4. Misguided – Part 2

1   *Report*, p. 160.

2   http://treaties.un.org/Pages/ViewDetails.aspx?mtdsg_no=IV-2&chapter=4&lang=en, accessed 25 June 2013.

3   *Report*, p. 160.

4   *Report*, pp. 49, 59, 60, 104, 130, 147, 164, 180.

5   The preamble to the Racial Discrimination Act 1975 states that the Act is in response to the UN Convention.

6   http://www.un.org/esa/socdev/unpfii/documents/DRIPS_en.pdf, accessed 7 July 2013.

7   Christian Kerr, "Uni body bans outspoken indigenous leader as 'unhealthy' for staff", *The Australian*, 19 July 2013, p. 3.

8   Howse, *Legally invisible*, p. 15.

9   As commentator Angela Shanahan recently lamented regarding restrictions of Church freedom by anti-discrimination laws: "Once upon a time in Australia we had implicit religious freedom; now we have to rely on exemptions." Shanahan was discussing an unseemly manoeuvre by Government Senate leader, Senator Mark Dreyfus, "Distracted MPs destroy religious freedom", *Weekend Australian*, 29-30 June 2013, Inquirer, p. 20.

10   *Report*, p. 34.

11   McPherson, M., L. Smith-Lovin and J. M. Cook (2001). Birds of a feather: Homophily in social networks. *Annual Review of Sociology* 27: 415-444.

12   Bishop, B. (2009). *The big sort: Why the clustering of like-minded America is tearing us apart*. Boston, Mariner Books.

13   Recent evidence of immigrants preferring to live among their own ethnic groups comes from real estate agents selling to overseas Chinese. Among other preferences such as good views and educational facilities, living near an established Chinese community was a recurring theme. "Chinese precise on where to buy", *The Australian*, 19-20 Oct. 2013, p. 7.

14   "Sydney should embrace Asia, says O'Farrell", *The Sydney Morning Herald*, 7 Nov. 2011, p. 1.

15   Mill, J. S. (1960). Chapter XVI: On nationality. *Representative government. Three essays by John Stuart Mill*. J. S. Mill. London, Oxford University Press: 380-88, p. 381.

16   Arendt, H. (1959). "Reflections of Little Rock [http://learningspaces.org/forgotten/little_rock1.pdf]." *Dissent*: 45-56, pp. 49, 51.

17   Calwell, A. A. (1978). *Be just and fear not*. Adelaide, Rigby, p. 118.

18   CERD General Recommendation 14: Definition of discrimination (Article 1, paragraph 1). http://www.unhchr.ch/tbs/doc.nsf/ %28Symbol%29/d7bd5d2bf71258aac12563ee004b639e? Opendocument, accessed 18 July 2013.

19   *Report*, Section 6.3, p. 160.

20   CERD article 1(4) states that special measures for racial groups are permissible, as long as they do not "lead to the maintenance of separate rights for different racial groups and that they shall not be continued after the objectives for which they were taken have been achieved".

21   *Report*, pp. v, 139.

22   International Convention on the Elimination of All Forms of Racial Discrimination, 1965, Preamble. http://treaties.un.org/Pages/ViewDetails.aspx?mtdsg_no=IV-2&chapter=4&lang=en.

23   Sarich, V. M. and F. Miele (2004). *Race: The reality of human differences*. Boulder, Colorado, Westview, pp. 170-77.

24   *Report*, p. 139.

25   The cited book, *The Concept of Race* does not turn up in online searches of Montagu's books. He did publish a paper by that title in 1962, in *American Anthropologist* 64(5:1), 919-28, which does not contain the quotation in the *Report* (p. 139). http://www.americanethnography.com/article.php? id=36#.UeipXKyTu_c, accessed 18 July 2013.

26   Montagu, M. F. A. (1997/1942). *Man's most dangerous myth: The fallacy of race*. New York, Columbia University Press. http://books.google.com.au/books? hl=en&lr=&id=tkHqP3vgYi4C&oi=fnd&pg=PA7&dq=ashley+monta gue&ots=apeK3A_wu9&sig=7b3MFARDGUWorU3MEErQbFCRRv M#v=onepage&q=Kleptomaniac&f=false, accessed 18 July 2013.

27   Diamond, J. (1997). *Guns, germs, and steel: The fates of human societies*. New York, W. W. Norton. Murray, C. (2004/2003). *Human accomplishment: The Pursuit of excellence in the arts and sciences, 800 B.C. to 1950*. New York, Harper Perennial.

28   Lynn, *Race differences in intelligence*.

29   Rushton, J. P. and A. R. Jensen (2005). "Thirty years of research on race differences in cognitive ability." *Psychology, Public Policy and Law* 11(2): 235-294.

30   Diamond, *Guns*, p. 20.

31   Eibl-Eibesfeldt, *Human ethology*, p. 572.

32   Eibl-Eibesfeldt, *Human ethology*, p. 572.

33   Montagu, *Man's most dangerous myth*, p. 45.

34   *Report*, p. 142.

35   Edwards, A. W. F. (2003). "Human genetic diversity: Lewontin's fallacy." *BioEssays* 25(8): 798-801.

36   (In outbred populations.) Salter, F. K. and H. Harpending (2012). "J. P. Rushton's theory of ethnic nepotism." Personality and Individual Differences http://www.sciencedirect.com/science/article/pii/S0191886912005569.
Harpending, H. (2002). "Kinship and population subdivision." *Population and Environment* 24(2): 141-147.

37   *Report*, p. 139.

38   Jews are described as a "race" in Herzl's address to the first Zionist Congress in Basel in 1897. Herzl, T. (1907-1903). *The Congress addresses of Theodor Herzl*. Miami, FL, HardPress, p. 7.

39   UN Convention on the Elimination of All Forms of Racial Discrimination, Article 1(1).

40   Also not mentioned in the curriculum: England, Britain/British, Christian/Christianity, First Fleet, Captain Cook, and Arthur Phillip. http://www.acara.edu.au/verve/_resources/Shape_of_the_Australian_Curriculum-__Civics_and_Citizenship_251012.pdf, accessed 19 July 2013;
Kevin Donnelly, "PM's school reform flawed", *The Australian*, 19 June 2013, p. 12.

41   Montagu, M. F. A. (1999/1953). *The natural superiority of women*, 5th edition, Sage.

42   Kaufmann, E. (2004). *The rise and fall of Anglo-America*. Cambridge, MA, Harvard University Press, p. 108.

43   Boas, F. (1912). *Changes in the bodily form of descendants of immigrants*. New York, Columbia University Press.
Sparks, C. S. and R. L. Jantz (2002). "A re-assessment of human cranial plasticity: Boas revisited." *Proceedings of the National Academy of Science www.pnas.org* 99(23): 14636-9.

44   Montagu, 1945/1942, *Man's most dangerous myth*, p. 4.

45   Lynn and Vanhanen, *IQ and the wealth of nations*.

46   http://www.nature.com/nature/journal/v449/n7165/full/449948a.html, accessed 26 July 2013.

47   Lynn, *Race differences in intelligence*, pp. 29-53.

48 E.g. Nicholas Wade (2006). *Before the dawn: Recovering the lost history of our ancestors*. New York, Penguin. Wade was the long-term science editor for the New York Times. In his book he discusses evolutionary scenarios for population differences in intelligence, paying attention to genetic difference between Europe and Australia (pp. 96-99).

49 Stocking, G. W. (1992). Anthropology as *Kulturkampf*: Science and politics in the career of Franz Boas. *The ethnographer's magic and other essays in the history of anthropology*. G. W. Stocking. Madison, WI, University of Wisconsin Press: 92-113, pp. 108-9.

50 Montagu, 1945/1942, *Man's most dangerous myth*, p. 82. http://archive.org/stream/mansmostdangerou032948mbp/mansm ostdangerou032948mbp_djvu.txt, accessed 26 July 2013.

51 Ashley Montagu papers, 1927-1999, http://amphilsoc.org/mole/view?docId=ead/Mss.Ms.Coll.109-ead.xml#d97490320e340955978792960, accessed 19 July 2013.

52 The left political climate of UNESCO from its early days was indicated by its first director-general, Julian Huxley, praising Lenin's propaganda methods for "overcoming the resistance of millions" in the context of UNESCO's educational mission. Huxley, J. S. (1947). *UNESCO: Its purpose and its philosophy*. Washington, DC, Public Affairs Press. Huxley was not a Communist. After WWII he criticised the Lamarckian theories and Stalinist politics of Trofim Lysenko.

53 Ashley Montagu papers, 1927-1999, http://amphilsoc.org/mole/view?docId=ead/Mss.Ms.Coll.109-ead.xml#d97490320e340955978792960, accessed 19 July 2013.

54 Maddocks, J. (1963). "Anglo-Saxon attitudes." *The New York Review of Books* 1(1).

55 Kaufmann, *Rise and Fall*, p. 151.

56 Snyderman, M. and S. Rothman (1988). *The IQ controversy: The media and public policy*. New York, Transaction Books.

57 Herrnstein, R. and C. Murray (1994). *The bell curve. Intelligence and class structure in American life*. New York, Free Press. Gottfredson, L. S. (1997). "Mainstream science on intelligence: An editorial with 52 signatories, history, and bibliography." *Intelligence* 24(1): 13-23.

58 Richwine, J. (2013). "Why can't we talk about IQ?" *Politico* http://www.politico.com/story/2013/08/opinion-jason-richwine-95353.html, accessed 19 Aug. 2013.

5. Misguided – Part 3

1   *Report*, pp. 234-9.

2   *Report*, pp. 234-9.

3   Errington, W. and P. van Onselen (2007). *John Winston Howard: The biography*. Melbourne, Melbourne University Press, p. 157.

4   Fitzgerald Inquiry, 1988, *Recommendations*. http://www.multiculturalaustralia.edu.au/library/media/Documen t/id/146.Immigration-A-Commitment-to-Australia-Recommendations.

     Errington and van Onselen, p. 156.

5   Blainey, G. (1984). *All for Australia*. North Ryde, Australia, Methuen Haynes, p. 167.

6   Stone, J. (2010). "Immigration policy: Our self-inflicted wounds." *Quadrant* 54:9 (http://www.quadrant.org.au/magazine/issue/2010/9/immigratio n-policy-our-self-inflicted-wounds).

7   "Party for father of the House", *The Age*, 23 Sept. 2003. http://www.theage.com.au/articles/2003/09/22/1064082929396. html, accessed 12 Aug. 2013.

8   Mark Leibler, "Stop the ugly politicking: this is a matter of life and death". http://www.smh.com.au/comment/stop-the-ugly-politicking-this-is-a-matter-of-life-and-death-20130802-2r5ex.html, accessed 27 Aug. 2013.

9   Mark Leibler's bio: http://www.abl.com.au/ablattach/leibler.pdf, accessed 27 Aug. 2013.

10   "Anger as One Nation members named", *The Sydney Morning Herald*, 10 July 1998, p. 1.

11   http://www.aijac.org.au/news/article/antisemitism-in-australia-2007-08, accessed 23 Aug. 2013.

12   Pearson worked with Leibler early in his career, and has referred to him as "my old Melbourne law mentor". http://www.theaustralian.com.au/national-affairs/pearson-tells-pm-give-us-first-vote/story-fn59niix-1225994541984, accessed 22 Aug. 2013.

13   *Report*, p. xix.

14   Leibler, "Racism still shadows our history".

15   Tony Koch, "Pearson yet to learn lessons of leadership", *The Weekend Australian*, 28-29 April, Inquirer, p. 18.

16   "Langton told to apologise for 'defamation'", *The Weekend Australian*, 17-18 Aug. 2013, p. 4.

17   Marcia Langton, "Why I continue to be inspired by Pearson", *The Weekend Australian*, 5-6 May 2012, Inquirer, p. 20.

18   Andrew Bolt, "Dividing us by race", *Herald Sun* (Melbourne), 20 Jan. 2012. http://blogs.news.com.au/heraldsun/andrewbolt/index.php/heraldsun/comments/dividing_us_by_race/, accessed 25 Oct. 2013.

19   "Historic Constitution vote over indigenous recognition facing hurdles", *op cit.*

20   "Ex-PM to receive Jerusalem Prize", *The Australian*, 1 Oct. 2013, p. 6.

21   Barack Obama's speech to students in Israel, 21 March 2013. http://www.telegraph.co.uk/news/worldnews/barackobama/9946851/Barack-Obamas-Israel-speech-transcript.html, accessed 31 July 2013.

22   Zeiger, A. "Russian-speakers who want to make aliya could need DNA test." *The Times of Israel.* 29 July 2013. http://www.timesofisrael.com/russian-speakers-who-want-to-immigrate-could-need-dna-test/, accessed 17 Aug. 2013.

23   Burke, *Reflections on revolution in France*, pp. 35, 36.

24   Frank Salter, 2012. "The war against human nature in the social sciences", Quadrant, in four parts: June, July-August, October, and November. http://www.quadrant.org.au/magazine/issue/2012/6/the-war-against-human-nature-in-the-social-sciences http://www.quadrant.org.au/magazine/issue/2012/7-8/the-war-against-human-nature-ii-gender-studies-part-1 http://www.quadrant.org.au/magazine/issue/2012/10/the-war-against-human-nature-iii-race-and-the-nation-in-the-media http://www.quadrant.org.au/magazine/issue/2012/11/the-war-against-human-nature-iii

25   Connor, M. (2005). *The invention of terra nullius: Historic and legal fictions on the foundation of Australia.* Sydney, Macleay Press. Especially Chapter 8, "*Terra nullius* and the intellectuals". For a rejoinder see Reynolds, H. (2006). "A new historic landscape? A response to Michael Connor's 'The Invention of Terra Nullius'." *The Monthly: Australian Politics, Society & Culture,* http://www.themonthly.com.au/issue/2006/may/1294984625/henry-reynolds/new-historic-landscape.

26   http://britishaustraliancommunity.com/wp/, accessed 4 July 2013. A recent book by a BAC member describes the demographic and political challenges facing Anglo-Celtic Australia. Alan James (2013). *New Britannia: The rise and decline of Anglo-Australia*. Melbourne.

27   Greg Sheridan, "People are fed up with continued growth in asylum-seeker numbers", *The Australian*, 13 June 2013, p. 12.

7. Section 18c, Multiculturalism and Power

1   The Act overrides state law because it invokes the federal foreign affairs power based on the Whitlam government signing the Orwellian UN Convention on the Elimination of All Forms of Racial Discrimination. See Salter, F. K. (2014). "The misguided case for indigenous recognition in the Constitution. Part II: Race and the culture wars [https://quadrant.org.au/magazine/2014/01-02/misguided-case-indigenous-recognition-constitution-part-ii/]." *Quadrant* 58(1): 32-40.

2   "Racial discrimination repeal likely to be scaled back", *The Australian*, 20 March 2014.

3   Dennis Shanahan (2014). "Fighting for freedom of speech eerily similar to a defence of bigotry", *The Australian*, 26 March 2014, pp. 1, 4.

4   "People have a right to be bigots, says Brandis", *The Australian*, 25 March 2014, p. 5.

     "Race act set for radical reshaping", *The Australian*, 18 March 2014, p. 6.

5   Grassby, A. J. (1984). *The tyranny of prejudice*. Melbourne, AE Press, p. 15.

6   Betts, K. (1999). *The great divide*. Sydney, Duffy & Snellgrove, p. 300.

7   "PM tackles backlash to bigot remark", *The Australian*, p. 4.

8   "People have a right to be bigots", *op cit*.

8. Biased Referendum Questions Crystallise Slowly

1   "Extension needed to heal race divisions", *The Australian*, 15 July 2014, p. 8.

Patricia Karvelas (2014). "Language barrier in nod for all people", *The Australian*, 19 June, p. 3. The earlier of these two reports is more detailed.

2   Karvelas, "Language barrier in nod for all people", op cit.

3   Chapters 3 to 5 in the present volume.

4   Patricia Karvelas (2014). "Peris to fight for referendum campaign funds", *The Australian*, 19 February, p. 6.

9. Shorten attempts to radicalise the referendum-council

1   "Shorten's referendum demands", *The Australian*, 4 August 2014, p. 2.   http://www.theaustralian.com.au/national-affairs/policy/bill-shortens-indigenous-referendum-demands/story-fn9hm1pm-1227012141049

11. Does reason matter? S18c and the referendum

1   Frank Salter, Multiculturalism: Divide and concur, *Quadrant Online*, 16 April 2014. http://quadrant.org.au/opinion/qed/2014/04/multiculturalism-divide-concur/

2   James Allan, Craven cave in on free speech, *The Australian*, 6 August 2014, p. 12. www.theaustralian.com.au/opinion/craven-cave-in-on-free-speech/news-story/23f5c38d4064fba84d17f7fadd169694

3   Tanya Hosch, Bring our people in from cold, *The Australian*, 5 August 2014, p. 10. www.theaustralian.com.au/national-affairs/opinion/bring-our-people-in-from-cold/news-story/d7512552e554009461ff7fb47be42cd5

4   Barry Maley, Abandon change to constitution, *The Australian*, 5 August 2014, p. 10.
http://www.theaustralian.com.au/opinion/abandon-change-to-constitution/news-story/05889b172417cd71d09d226bafd52f8a

5   Salter, F. K. (2017/2010). The misguided advocates of open borders. In F. K. Salter (Ed.), *The war on human nature in Australia's political culture* (pp. 114-127): Social Technologies, Sydney.

12. 'Recognise' the retreat

1   Dennis Shanahan (2014). Proposal to delay referendum. *The Australian*, 12 Sept. http://www.theaustralian.com.au/national-affairs/indigenous/proposal-to-delay-referendum/news-story/284b8eba2102a3a9aff231ea72afed6c

2   PM flags delay on indigenous referendum. *The Australian*, 6 Dec. 2014. http://www.theaustralian.com.au/news/latest-news/pm-flags-delay-on-indigenous-referendum/news-story/702f984e42ef31d840658a77be0fc6a0

3   Patricia Karvelas (2014). Noel Pearson finds way to salvage referendum, advance his people. *The Australian*, 10 Sept. http://www.theaustralian.com.au/national-affairs/indigenous/noel-pearson-finds-way-to-salvage-referendum-advance-his-people/news-story/bcb7b6eae3fa102f307d7a77d80ca93c

4   Damien Freeman (2014). Addressing Aboriginal disadvantage–that's what I call a defining moment. *The Australian*, 6 Sept. http://www.theaustralian.com.au/opinion/addressing-aboriginal-disadvantage-thats-what-i-call-a-defining-moment/news-story/c42b4cdd28ef7e4c4fe3ff2bc000ccd7

5   Paul Kelly (2014). To succeed, indigenous recognition referendum must be handled deftly. *The Australian*, 10 Sept. http://www.theaustralian.com.au/opinion/columnists/paul-kelly/to-succeed-indigenous-recognition-referendum-must-be-handled-deftly/news-story/cd0fbee39cde82ac00297ecc9fa4bd6d

6   Wesley Aird (2014). Improve education, employment and community safety for indigenous Australians. *The Australian*, 6 Sept. http://www.theaustralian.com.au/opinion/improve-education-employment-and-community-safety-for-indigenous-australians/news-story/1203fdd4094c508738ba7682de3960dd

13. Prisoner Abbott: Referendum Developments

1   http://www.theaustralian.com.au/national-affairs/indigenous/warren-mundine-treaty-needed-with-each-first-nation/news-story/4ae32087476d1b259f3d415d70a71564

2   Simon Cullen (2013). Abbott rubbishes Wilders' views on Islam. *ABC News*, 20 Feb. www.abc.net.au/news/2013-02-20/abbott-rubbishes-wilders27s-views-on-islam/4529514

3   http://www.liberal.org.au/latest-news/2012/09/20/tony-abbott-speech-vote-thanks-inaugural-australian-multicultural-council

4   Patricia Karvelas (2012). Millions ready to back Recognise campaign for constitutional change. *The Australian*, 20 Sept. http://www.liberal.org.au/latest-news/2012/09/20/tony-abbott-speech-vote-thanks-inaugural-australian-multicultural-council

5   Patricia Karvelas (2014). Nation wants equality, not ready to vote. *The Australian*, 20 Sept. http://www.theaustralian.com.au/national-affairs/indigenous/nation-wants-equality-not-ready-to-vote/news-story/452e665f2fce82cff8ee8e7ede85fff4

6   Patricia Karvelas (2014). Republic foes Kerry Jones and Tom Keneally join hands to recognize past. *The Australian*, 4 Dec. http://www.theaustralian.com.au/national-affairs/indigenous/republic-foes-kerry-jones-and-tom-keneally-join-hands-to-recognise-past/news-story/6371c2a5bb82b0606d8f43450d8d8217

7   Patricia Karvelas (2013). Change needs a conservative: Noel Pearson. *The Australian*, 26 Aug. http://www.theaustralian.com.au/national-affairs/in-depth/change-needs-a-conservative-noel-pearson/news-story/8b9441d11fb2b61ed9903318aab4e5f0

8   Johns, G. (Ed.) (2014). *Recognise what? Arguments to acknowledge Aborigines, but not recognise Aboriginal culture or rights, in the Australian Constitution*. Ballarat: Connor Court.

9   Barry Maley (2014). Abandon change to constitution. *The Australian*, 5 Aug. http://www.theaustralian.com.au/opinion/abandon-change-to-constitution/news-story/05889b172417cd71d09d226bafd52f8a

10   John Roskam (2014). Indigenous recognition will hand power to judges. *The Australian*, 3 Nov. http://www.theaustralian.com.au/opinion/indigenous-recognition-will-hand-power-to-judges/news-story/c913f56b2821200ebfb9259c68a60cea

11 David Flint and Jai Martinkovits (2014). Heeding the people's voice. *The Australian*, 4 Dec. http://www.theaustralian.com.au/opinion/heeding-the-peoples-voice/news-story/6c508aaf19af1101b8f3145f99cc68e1

12 Patricia Karvelas (2014). I'll sweat blood for 2017 indigenous referendum vote, says Tony Abbott. *The Australian*, 12 Dec. http://www.theaustralian.com.au/national-affairs/in-depth/journey-to-recognition/ill-sweat-blood-for-2017-indigenous-referendum-vote-says-tony-abbott/news-story/a196cce08d1b75024fcce01c30e8e2bf

13 Frank Salter (2014). Section 18c, multiculturalism, and power. Chapter 7 of this volume.

14 Karvelas (2014). I'll sweat blood, op cit.

15 Noel Pearson (2014). 'Time to bring us into the nation' through constitutional recognition. *The Australian*, 1 Sept. http://www.theaustralian.com.au/opinion/columnists/noel-pearson/time-to-bring-us-into-the-nation-through-constitutional-recognition/news-story/624b19f117e0bbb9c756fefdf7905bf9

16 Sheridan, G. (2014). Constitutional change will divide not unite the nation. *The Australian*, 20 Sept. http://www.theaustralian.com.au/opinion/columnists/constitutional-change-will-divide-not-unite-the-nation/story-e6frg76f-1227064539257

17 Noel Pearson, 2011, *Up from the mission: Selected writings*, Collingwood, Victoria: Schwartz Media, p. 337.

14. Why the business council of Australia?

1 Rick Morton (2015). Chance for indigenous constitutional recognition 'may be squandered'. *The Australian*, 2 Feb. http://www.theaustralian.com.au/national-affairs/in-depth/journey-to-recognition/chance-for-indigenous-constitutional-recognition-may-be-squandered/news-story/6a087f2ee1bbde3c3c77c69a5e48b826

16. Recognise campaign in disarray

1   Noel Pearson (2011). Constitutional reform crucial to indigenous wellbeing. *The Australian*, 24 Dec. http://www.theaustralian.com.au/national-affairs/opinion/constitutional-reform-crucial-to-indigenous-wellbeing/news-story/8fdfea100f068724be537cc10f0c878f

2   Salter, F. K. (2017/2014). *The war on human nature in Australia's political culture*: Social Technologies.

3   Noel Pearson (2015). This is country country too. *The Australian*, 14 April. http://www.theaustralian.com.au/opinion/columnists/noel-pearson/this-is-our-country-too/news-story/87b8b3a9ab79ce475699905935e042eb8

4   Geoffrey Partington (2015). Letter to the editor. *The Australian*, 16 April. http://www.theaustralian.com.au/opinion/letters/letters-declaration-rather-than-referendum-would-be-best/news-story/96909e0039a6d0122f4f76d4bbb9d3fd

5   James Paterson (2015). No place for laws aimed at race. *The Australian*, 16 April. http://www.theaustralian.com.au/opinion/no-place-for-laws-aimed-at-race/news-story/0146e6b2e63a6de8ab1e660a3a41f5a2

6   Frank Salter (2014). Multiculturalism: Divide and concur. *Quadrant Online*, 16 April. www.quadrant.org.au/opinion/qed/2014/04/multiculturalism-divide-concur/

7   Sheridan, G. (2014). Constitutional change will divide not unite the nation. *The Australian*, 20 Sept. http://www.theaustralian.com.au/opinion/columnists/constitutional-change-will-divide-not-unite-the-nation/story-e6frg76f-1227064539257

17. The Pearson Factor

1   Emma Alberici (2015). Interview: Cape York indigenous leader Noel Pearson, 6 July. http://www.abc.net.au/lateline/interview-cape-york-indigenous-leader-noel-pearson/6599764

2   Noel Pearson (2013). Whitlam oration: In honour of the old man, 13 Nov. http://australianpolitics.com/2013/11/13/noel-pearson-whitlam-oration.html

3   Reproduced in chapters 3, 4 and 5 in the present volume.

4   Hirschfeld, L. A. (1996). *Race in the making. Cognition, culture, and the child's construction of human kinds*. Cambridge, MA, MIT Press.

5   Salter, F. K. (2007). *On genetic interests : Family, ethnicity, and humanity in an age of mass migration*. New Brunswick, N.J., Transaction Publishers.

6   Salter, F. K. (2017/2010). Misguided advocates of open borders. Chapter 5 (pp. 114-127), *The war on human nature*, Social Technologies.

7   Chapter 4 of the present volume.

8   Sarah Martin (2015). Referendum 'in danger' of no campaign, *The Australian*, 5 June, p. 8.
http://www.theaustralian.com.au/national-affairs/indigenous/indigenous-referendum-in-danger-of-no-campaign/story-fn9hm1pm-1227383572838

18. Now It's Indigenous-Only Constitutional Conventions

1   Rebecca Puddy, "Recognition show 'back on the rails'" *The Australian* 21 August 2015, p. 7.
http://www.theaustralian.com.au/national-affairs/indigenous/recognition-show-back-on-the-rails/story-fn9hm1pm-1227492174151

2   Salter, F. K. (2014). Multiculturalism: Divide and concur. *Quadrant Online*. 28 March.
http://quadrant.org.au/opinion/qed/2014/04/multiculturalism-divide-concur/
Salter, F. K. (2014, 28 March). Section 18C, multiculturalism and power. *Quadrant Online*, 28 March:
http://quadrant.org.au/opinion/qed/2014/03/section-18c-multiculturalism-power/.

3   Salter, F. K. (2012). "The war against human nature III-2: Australia and the national question, part II: Race and the nation in the universities." *Quadrant* 56(11 (491)): 36-44.
http://www.quadrant.org.au/magazine/issue/2012/11/the-war-against-human-nature-iii

19. Gillard's Ghost: The new Referendum Council

1   "Referendum Council". Joint press release by the Prime Minister
     and Leader of the Opposition, 7 Dec. 2015.
     https://www.pm.gov.au/media/2015-12-07/referendum-council

2   Council Membership:
     https://www.pm.gov.au/sites/default/files/media/referendum_cou
     ncil_membership.pdf

3   http://www.law.unsw.edu.au/news/2015/04/unsw-human-rights-
     lawyer-professor-megan-davis-has-been-elected-chair-united-
     nations

4   Salter, F. K. (2014). "The misguided case for indigenous recognition
     in the Constitution. Part II: Race and the culture wars
     [https://quadrant.org.au/magazine/2014/01-02/misguided-case-
     indigenous-recognition-constitution-part-ii/]." *Quadrant* 58(1): 32-
     40. http://quadrant.org.au/magazine/2014/03/misguided-case-
     indigenous-recognition-part-iii/

www.ingramcontent.com/pod-product-compliance
Lightning Source LLC
Chambersburg PA
CBHW070117260726
48658CB00001B/139